The
Treasure Chest

The Treasure Chest

MEMORABLE WORDS OF
WISDOM AND INSPIRATION

HarperSanFrancisco
A Division of HarperCollins*Publishers*

Every effort has been made to ensure that permission has been obtained
for use of prose excerpts greater than 350 words in length and poetry
excerpts of more than two lines. If any required acknowledgments have been
omitted or any rights overlooked, please notify the publishers and omissions
will be rectified in future editions. For acknowledgments of permission
to reprint copyrighted material, see page 224. Occasional quotations are
from an unknown source.

The first edition of *The Treasure Chest* was compiled by Charles L. Wallis.

This edition of *The Treasure Chest* has been compiled by Brian Culhane
and produced by Marquand Books, Inc.
Designed by Susan E. Kelly

Library of Congress Cataloging-in-Publication Data
The treasure chest : memorable words of wisdom and inspiration /
[compiled by Brian Culhane]. — 1st ed.
p.   cm.
Includes index.
ISBN 0-06-069246-4 (cloth : alk. paper)
1. Conduct of life—Quotations, maxims, etc. I. Culhane, Brian.
BJ1548.T74   1995
081—dc20   95-12745

95 96 97 98 99 MAR 10 9 8 7 6 5 4 3 2 1

Contents

Preface

~

"A WORD FITLY SPOKEN," said Solomon, "is like apples of gold in pictures of silver." Such a word is a recipe for happiness, a challenging guidepost along our journey through life, a bright star to which we may hitch our wagon, or perhaps a vine-covered arbor under which we may find peace, poise, and contentment.

The words quoted in this book reflect the experiences of our common life and by an uncommon grace of expression mirror what most of us have thought or felt or aspire to think and feel. To inspire means literally to breathe into and infuse with life. Inspiring words influence our thinking, enliven our sensitivity to life's meanings, arouse us from lethargy, and exalt us by strengthening the heart and restoring the soul. A perennially vivacious sentiment gives breadth of vision and stretches the heart's sympathies.

This abundant harvest of the wisdom of many centuries follows no predetermined editorial pattern or arbitrary method of choice. In many gardens of prose and verse I have plucked here a red rose and there a golden apple. What I have enjoyed reading I hope others will find to be equally delightful. Where I have found refreshing spring water I hope others will dip their cups. On some mountain height I have moved aside so that others may also share the view of a mind-expanding horizon.

— CHARLES L. WALLIS

Publisher's Note to the New Edition
This new edition contains four hundred new selections, with an equal number carried over from the first edition compiled by Charles L. Wallis. The Publishers express their gratitude to Brian Culhane and Marquand Books for their assistance in producing the new edition.

Achievement

It is never too late to be
what you might have been.

George Eliot

Achievement

Love yourself first and everything else falls into line. You really have to love yourself to get anything done in this world.

— LUCILLE BALL

♦

That man is a success who has lived well, laughed often and loved much; who has gained the respect of intelligent men and the love of children; who has filled his niche and accomplished his task; who leaves the world better than he found it, whether by an improved poppy, a perfect poem or a rescued soul; who never lacked appreciation of earth's beauty or failed to express it; who looked for the best in others and gave the best he had.

— ROBERT LOUIS STEVENSON

♦

I have always preferred having wings to having things.

— PATRICIA SCHROEDER

♦

Haunted from my early youth by the transitoriness and pathos of life, I was aware that it was not enough to say "I am doing no harm," I ought to be testing myself daily, and asking myself what I am really achieving.

— MARGOT ASQUITH

I do not want to die . . . until I have faithfully made the most of my talent and cultivated the seed that was placed in me until the last small twig has grown.

— KÄTHE KOLLWITZ

♦

Lincoln's Road to the White House
Failed in business in 1831.
Defeated for Legislature in 1832.
Second failure in business in 1833.
Suffered nervous breakdown in 1836.
Defeated for Speaker in 1838.
Defeated for Elector in 1840.
Defeated for Congress in 1843.
Defeated for Congress in 1848.
Defeated for Senate in 1855.
Defeated for Vice President in 1856.
Defeated for Senate in 1858.
Elected President in 1860.

♦

That's one small step for a man, one giant leap for mankind.

— NEIL ARMSTRONG
(first step on the moon, July 20, 1969)

♦

If one advances confidently in the direction of his dreams, and endeavors to live the life which he has imagined, he will meet with a success unexpected in common hours.

— HENRY DAVID THOREAU

The measure of success is not whether you have a tough problem to deal with, but whether it's the same problem you had last year.

— JOHN FOSTER DULLES

♦

Road to Success

Throw away all ambition beyond that of doing the day's work well. The travelers on the road to success live in the present, heedless of taking thought for the morrow. Live neither in the past nor in the future, but let each day's work absorb your entire energies, and satisfy your widest ambition.

— WILLIAM OSLER

♦

I think self-awareness is probably the most important thing towards being a champion.

— BILLY JEAN KING

♦

Mozart died in his six- and thirtieth year. Raphael at the same age. Byron only a little older. But all these had perfectly fulfilled their missions; and it was time for them to depart, that other people might still have something to do in a world made to last a long while.

— JOHANN WOLFGANG VON GOETHE

Success

Before God's footstool to confess
 A poor soul knelt and bowed his head.
 "I failed," he wailed. The Master said,
"Thou didst thy best — that is success."

♦

Appreciation

All human beings have failings, all human beings have needs and temptations and stresses. Men and women who live together through long years get to know one another's failings; but they also come to know what is worthy of respect and admiration in those they live with and in themselves. If at the end one can say, "This man used to the limit the powers that God granted him; he was worthy of love and respect and of the sacrifices of many people, made in order that he might achieve what he deemed to be his task," then that life has been lived well and there are no regrets.

— ELEANOR ROOSEVELT

♦

You never get promoted when no one else knows your current job. The best basis for being advanced is to organize yourself out of every job you're put in. Most people are advanced because they're pushed up from people underneath them rather than pulled by the top.

— DONALD DAVID

Success is to be measured not so much
by the position that one has reached
in life as by the obstacles which he has
overcome while trying to succeed.

— BOOKER T. WASHINGTON

Recipe for Greatness
To bear up under loss;
To fight the bitterness of defeat and
    the weakness of grief;
To be victor over anger;
To smile when tears are close;
To resist disease and evil men and
    base instincts;
To hate hate and to love love;
To go on when it would seem good
    to die;
To look up with unquenchable faith in
    something ever more about to be.
That is what any man can do, and
    be great.

— ZANE GREY

I think that it is a great achievement to
put a man on the moon. But to put a
man on the earth — that is even more.

— HARRISON SALISBURY

Four steps to achievement:
Plan purposefully. Prepare prayerfully.
Proceed positively. Pursue persistently.

— WILLIAM A. WARD

I don't know the key to success, but
the key to failure is trying to please
everybody.

— BILL COSBY

If we hope to live not just from moment
to moment, but in true consciousness
of our existence, then our greatest need
and most difficult achievement is to find
meaning in our lives.

— BRUNO BETELHEIM

Even the woodpecker owes his success
to the fact that he uses his head and
keeps pecking away until he finishes
the job he starts.

— COLEMAN COX

My mother drew a distinction between
achievement and success. She said that
"achievement is the knowledge that you
have studied and worked hard and done
the best that is in you. Success is being
praised by others, and that's nice too,
but not as important or satisfying."
Always aim for achievement and forget
about success.

— HELEN HAYES

Show me a thoroughly satisfied man,
and I will show you a failure.

— THOMAS A. EDISON

Action

All our actions take their hue
from the complexion of the heart,
as landscapes their variety from light.

Francis Bacon

The life of wisdom must be a life of contemplation combined with action.

— M. SCOTT PECK

♦

It is well with me only when I have a chisel in my hand.

— MICHELANGELO

♦

Conditional Freedom
God frees our souls, not from service, not from duty, but into service and into duty, and he who mistakes the purpose of his freedom mistakes the character of his freedom. He who thinks that he is being released from the work, and not set free in order that he may accomplish that work, mistakes the condition into which his soul is invited to enter.

— PHILLIPS BROOKS

♦

All mankind is divided into three classes: those that are immovable, those that are movable, and those that move.

— BENJAMIN FRANKLIN

♦

All the beautiful sentiments in the world weigh less than a single lovely action.

— JAMES RUSSELL LOWELL

Written in Actions
No one can write his real religious life with pen or pencil. It is written only in actions, and its seal is our character, not our orthodoxy. Whether we, our neighbor, or God is the judge, absolutely the only value of our religious life to ourselves or to anyone is what it fits us for and enables us to do.

— WILFRED T. GRENFELL

♦

As-If Principle: If you want a quality, act as if you already had it.

— WILLIAM JAMES

♦

Tears and weeping are mere self-indulgence if, in the final analysis, we don't act to find and implement alternatives to hatred, injustice and violence in all forms.

— MARIREAD CORRIGAN MAGUIRE

♦

Man's actions are the picture book of his creeds.

— RALPH WALDO EMERSON

♦

All that is essential for the triumph of evil is that good men do nothing.

— EDMUND BURKE

He that leaveth nothing to Chance will do few things ill, but he will do very few things.

—GEORGE, LORD HALIFAX

♦

The Ways
To every man there openeth
A Way, and Ways, and a Way.
And the High Soul climbs the
    High Way,
And the Low Soul gropes the Low,
And in between, on the misty flats,
The rest drift to and fro.
But to every man there openeth
A High Way, and a Low.
And every man decideth
The way his soul shall go.

—JOHN OXENHAM

♦

You can't build a reputation on what you're going to do.

—HENRY FORD

♦

The problem is not . . . to suppress change, which cannot be done, but to manage it. If we opt for rapid change in certain sectors of life we can consciously attempt to build stability zones elsewhere.

—ALVIN TOFFLER

The bitterest tears shed over graves are for words left unsaid and deeds left undone.

—HARRIET BEECHER STOWE

♦

As a Man Soweth
We must not hope to be mowers,
    And to gather the ripe gold ears,
Unless we have first been sowers
    And watered the furrows with tears.
It is not just as we take it,
    This mystical world of ours,
Life's field will yield as we make it
    A harvest of thorns or of flowers.

—JOHANN WOLFGANG
VON GOETHE

♦

Even if you're on the right track, you'll get run over if you just sit there.

—WILL ROGERS

♦

In war or in peace the naked fact remains the same. We are given one life, we have one span to live it. We can wait for circumstances to make up their minds or we can decide to act, and in acting, live.

—OMAR BRADLEY

♦

You can plan events, but if they go according to your plan they are not events.

—JOHN BERGER

Life is not made up of great
   sacrifices and duties,
But of little things; in
   which smiles
And kindness and small
   obligations,
Given habitually, are
   what win and
Preserve the heart and
   secure comfort.

— HUMPHRY DAVY

◆

In his own way each man must struggle,
lest the moral law become a far-off
abstraction utterly separated from his
active life.

— JANE ADDAMS

◆

A man who has to be convinced to act
before he acts is *not* a man of action. It's
as if a tennis player before returning the
ball began to question himself as to the
physical and moral value of tennis. You
must act just as you breathe.

— GEORGES CLEMENCEAU

◆

Let your doing be an exercise, not an
exhibition.

— JEAN TOOMER

It is the mark of a good action that it
appears inevitable in retrospect.

— ROBERT LOUIS STEVENSON

◆

Young people say, What is the sense of
our small effort? They cannot see that
they must lay one brick at a time, take
one step at a time; we can be responsible
only for the one action at the present
moment. But we can beg for an increase
of love in our hearts that will vitalize
and transform all our individual actions,
and know that God will take them and
multiply them, as Jesus multiplied the
loaves and fishes.

— DOROTHY DAY

◆

Ideas not coupled with action never
become bigger than the brain cells they
occupied.

— ARNOLD H. GLASOW

◆

Each morning sees some task begun,
Each morning sees its close.
Something attempted, something done,
Has earned a night's repose.

— HENRY WADSWORTH
    LONGFELLOW

Adversity

We shall steer safely through every storm,
so long as our heart is right,
our intention fervent, our courage steadfast,
and our trust fixed on God.

St. Francis of Sales

Adversity, if for no other reason, is of benefit, since it is sure to bring a season of sober reflection. Men see clearer at such times. Storms purify the atmosphere.

— HENRY WARD BEECHER

♦

Think or Worry?
You can think about your problems or you can worry about them, and there is a vast difference between the two. Worry is thinking that has turned toxic. It is jarring music that goes round and round and never comes to either climax or conclusion. Thinking works its way through problems to conclusions and decisions; worry leaves you in a state of tensely suspended animation. When you worry, you go over the same ground endlessly and come out the same place you started. Thinking makes progress from one place to another; worry remains static. The problem of life is to change worry into thinking and anxiety into creative action.

— HAROLD B. WALKER

♦

There is in every true woman's heart a spark of heavenly fire, which lies dormant in the broad daylight of prosperity; but which kindles up, and beams and blazes in the dark hour of adversity.

— WASHINGTON IRVING

I am an old man and have known a great many troubles, but most of them have never happened.

— MARK TWAIN

♦

All problems become smaller if you don't dodge them but confront them. Touch a thistle timidly, and it pricks you; grasp it boldly, and its spines crumble.

— WILLIAM S. HALSEY

♦

Nothing happens to anybody which he is not fitted by nature to bear.

— MARCUS AURELIUS

♦

Giving Back
Some people have a belief that every tree, when it burns, gives back the colors that went into its making—they see in the flaming logs the red of many sunsets, the purple of early dawn, the silver of moonrise and the sparkle of stars. So it is with us: what we have accepted into our hearts and made a permanent part of ourselves is given back in times of trials.

— FULTON J. SHEEN

♦

In the hour of adversity be not without hope
For crystal rain falls from black clouds.

— NIZAMI

Remembrance
Undaunted by Decembers,
The sap is faithful yet.
The giving earth remembers
And only men forget.

— JOHN G. NEIHARDT

Man is never helped in his suffering by
what he thinks for himself, but only by
revelation of a wisdom greater than his
own. It is this which lifts him out of his
distress.

— C. G. JUNG

It is in the whole process of meeting and
solving problems that life has meaning.
Problems are the cutting edge that dis-
tinguishes between success and failure.
Problems call forth our courage and our
wisdom; indeed, they create our courage
and our wisdom. It is only because of
problems that we grow mentally and
spiritually. It is through the pain of confronting and resolving problems that
we learn.

— M. SCOTT PECK

Only in winter can you tell which trees
are truly green. Only when the winds of
adversity blow can you tell whether an
individual or a country has courage and
steadfastness.

— JOHN F. KENNEDY

Never a tear bedims the eye
That time and patience will not dry.

— BRET HARTE

All sorrows can be borne if you put
them into a story or tell a story about
them.

— ISAK DINESEN

Change
We do not succeed in changing things
according to our desire, but gradually
our desire changes. The situation that
we hoped to change because it was intolerable becomes unimportant. We
have not managed to surmount the ob-
stacle, as we were absolutely determined
to do, but life has taken us round it, led
us past it, and then if we turn round to
gaze at the remote past, we can barely
catch sight of it, so imperceptible has
it become.

— MARCEL PROUST

I do not believe that true optimism can
come about except through tragedy.

— MADELEINE L'ENGLE

Birds sing after a storm; why shouldn't
people feel free to delight in whatever
remains to them?

— ROSE KENNEDY

A man of character finds a special attractiveness in difficulty, since it is only by coming to grips with difficulty that he can realize his potentialities.

— CHARLES DE GAULLE

♦

Life is to be lived, not controlled, and humanity is won by continuing to play in face of certain defeat.

— RALPH ELLISON

♦

One by One

In the old *McGuffey's Reader* is a story about the clock that had been running for a long, long time on the mantelpiece. One day the clock began to think about how many times during the year ahead it would have to tick. It counted up the seconds — 31,536,000 in the year — and the old clock just got too tired and said, "I can't do it," and stopped right there. When somebody reminded the clock that it did not have to tick the 31,536,000 seconds all at one time, but rather one by one, it began to run again and everything was all right.

— NENIEN C. MCPHERSON, JR.

♦

The mark of your ignorance is the depth of your belief in injustice and tragedy. What the caterpillar calls the end of the world, the master calls a butterfly.

— RICHARD BACH

The Old and the New

Let this New Year be the beginning of a new life in each of us wherein "old things are passed away." Not the old thoughts, of course, which are still true: but those that remain to nurse and encourage our prejudices. Not the old emotions that are filled with kindness: but all anger and bitter feeling and railing. Not the old reverence for the authority of God: but all fears born of our unworthy service apart from him.

Not the old gracious ministries that blessed mankind: but the harsh words, the suspicious looks, the clenched hands, and unwilling feet. Not the old habits that keep us in the straight way: but the new fashions that make us unmindful of those things which hold life together in the unity of good manners. Not the old friends who grow more beloved each year because their worth is better appreciated: but the new associations made from mercenary motives.

Let all blessed old things stay, but let the clutter of our heads and hearts be removed, that new inspirations and new affections may come in to gladden our lives.

— CHESTER BURGE EMERSON

♦

We could never learn to be brave and patient, if there were only joy in the world.

— HELEN KELLER

Age

I shall grow old, but never lose life's zest,
Because the road's last turn will be the best.

Henry van Dyke

In the central place of every heart there is a recording chamber; so long as it receives messages of beauty, hope, cheer, and courage, so long are you young. When the wires are all down and your heart is covered with the snows of pessimism and the ice of cynicism, then only are you grown old.

— DOUGLAS MAC ARTHUR

♦

I have only managed to live so long by carrying no hatreds.

— WINSTON CHURCHILL

♦

Mellowness

I like spring, but it is too young. I like summer, but it is too proud. So I like best of all autumn, because its leaves are a little yellow, its tone mellower, its colors richer, and it is tinged a little with sorrow. Its golden richness speaks not of the innocence of spring, nor of the power of summer, but of the mellowness and kindly wisdom of approaching age. It knows the limitations of life and is content.

— LIN YUTANG

♦

To be seventy years young is sometimes far more cheerful and hopeful than to be forty years old.

— OLIVER WENDELL HOLMES

Life Begins at Seventy

Between the ages of 70 and 83 Commodore Vanderbilt added about 100 millions of his fortune.

Kant at 74 wrote his *Anthropology, Metaphysics of Ethics,* and *Strife of the Faculties.*

Tintoretto at 74 painted the vast *Paradise,* a canvas 74 feet by 30.

Verdi at 74 produced his masterpiece, *Othello;* at 80, *Falstaff,* and at 85, the famous *Ave Maria, Stabet Mater,* and *Te Deum.*

Lamarck at 78 completed his great zoological work, *The Natural History of the Invertebrates.*

Oliver Wendell Holmes at 79 wrote *Over the Teacups.*

Cato at 80 began the study of Greek.

Goethe at 80 completed *Faust.*

Tennyson at 83 wrote "Crossing the Bar."

Titian at 98 painted his historic picture of the Battle of Lepanto.

— THE GOLDEN BOOK

Every time I think that I'm getting old, and gradually going to the grave, something else happens.

— LILLIAN CARTER

◆

I have enjoyed greatly the second blooming that comes when you finish the life of the emotions and of personal relations; and suddenly find — at the age of fifty, say — that a whole new life has opened before you, filled with things you can think about, study, or read about. . . . It is as if a fresh sap of ideas and thoughts was rising in you.

— AGATHA CHRISTIE

◆

To Old Age. I see in you the estuary that enlarges and spreads itself grandly as it pours in the Great Sea.

— WALT WHITMAN

◆

from Rabbi Ben Ezra
Grow old along with me!
The best is yet to be,
The last of life, for which the first
   was made:
Our times are in his hand
Who saith, "A whole I planned,
Youth shows but half; trust God:
   see all, nor be afraid!"

— ROBERT BROWNING

I am spending delightful afternoons in my garden, watching everything living around me. As I grow older, I feel everything departing, and I love everything with more passion.

— EMILE ZOLA

◆

Diagnosis
On his eightieth birthday, John Quincy Adams responded to a query concerning his well-being by saying: "John Quincy Adams is well. But the house in which he lives at present is becoming dilapidated. It is tottering upon its foundation. Time and the seasons have nearly destroyed it. Its roof is pretty well worn out. Its walls are much shattered and it trembles with every wind. I think John Quincy Adams will have to move out of it soon. But he himself is quite well, quite well."

◆

Mailer never had a particular age — he carried different ages within him like different models of his experience: parts of him were eighty-one years old, fifty-seven, forty-eight, thirty-six, nineteen, et cetera, et cetera — he now went back abruptly from fifty-seven to thirty-six.

— NORMAN MAILER

Perhaps middle-age is, or should be,
a period of shedding shells; the shell
of ambition, the shell of material accu-
mulations and possessions, the shell of
the ego.

— ANNE MORROW LINDBERGH

♦

Inspiration
It is said that hope goes with youth; but
I fancy that hope is the last gift given
to man, and the only gift not given to
youth. For youth the end of every epi-
sode is the end of the world. But the
power of hoping through everything,
the knowledge that the soul survives
its adventures — that great inspiration
comes to the middle-aged.

— GILBERT KEITH CHESTERTON

♦

The heyday of a woman's life is the
shady side of fifty, when the vital forces
heretofore expanded in other ways are
garnered in the brain, when their
thoughts and sentiments flow out in
broader channels, when philanthropy
takes the place of family selfishness, and
when from the depths of poverty and
suffering the wail of humanity grows as
pathetic to their ears as once was the cry
of their own children.

— ELIZABETH CADY STANTON

The evening of the year brings with it
its lamp.

— JOSEPH JOUBERT

♦

I never expected to have, in my sixties,
the happiness that passed me by in my
twenties.

— C. S. LEWIS

♦

His Words at Ninety
The riders in a race do not stop short
when they reach the goal. There is a
little finishing canter before they come
to a standstill. There is time to hear the
kind voice of friends and to say to one's
self: "The work is done." But just as one
says that, the answer comes: "The race is
over, but the work never is done while
the power to work remains." The canter
that brings you to a standstill need not
be only coming to rest. It cannot be
while you still live. For to live is to function. That is all there is in living.

— OLIVER WENDELL HOLMES, JR.

♦

That tree is very old, but I never saw
prettier blossoms on it than it now
bears. That tree grows new wood each
year. Like that apple tree, I try to grow
a little new wood each year.

— HENRY WADSWORTH
LONGFELLOW

The Best Is Yet to Come
Though I am growing old, I maintain
that the best part is yet to come—the
time when one may see things more
dispassionately and know oneself and
others more truly, and perhaps be able
to do more, and in religion rest centered
in a few simple truths. I do not want to
ignore the other side, that one will not
be able to see so well or walk so far or
read so much. But there may be more
peace within more communion with
God, more real light instead of distrac-
tion about many things, better relations
with others, fewer mistakes.

— BENJAMIN JOWETT

♦

To me, old age is always fifteen years
older than I am.

— BERNARD M. BARUCH
(upon observing his 85th birthday)

♦

In spite of illness, in spite even of the
arch-enemy sorrow, one can remain alive
long past the usual date of disintegration
if one is unafraid of change, insatiable in
intellectual curiosity, interested in big
things, and happy in small ways.

— EDITH WHARTON

♦

For years I wanted to be older, and now
I am.

— MARGARET ATWOOD

When I was younger I could remember
anything, whether it happened or not,
but I am getting old and soon shall remember only the latter.

— MARK TWAIN

♦

Fulfillment
To fulfill the dreams of one's youth; that
is the best that can happen to a man.
No worldly success can take the place
of that.

— WILLA CATHER

♦

The last concert of my career was
the one I gave at the Wigmore Hall
in London for the benefit of the hall,
which was in danger of being demol-
ished. My concert was to be an example
to other artists in order to save the old
endangered place. As for myself, it was
a symbolic gesture; it was in this hall
that I had given my first recital in London and playing there for the last time
in my life made me think of my whole
career in the form of a sonata. The first
movement represented the struggles of
my youth, the following andante for
the beginning of a more serious aspect
of my talent, a scherzo represented well
the unexpected great success, and the
finale turned out to be a wonderful
moving end.

— ARTUR RUBINSTEIN

When You Are Old

When you are old and grey and full of sleep,
And nodding by the fire, take down this book,
And slowly read, and dream of the soft look
Your eyes had once, and of their shadows deep;

How many loved your moments of glad grace,
And loved your beauty with love false or true,
But one man loved the pilgrim soul in you,
And loved the sorrows of your changing face;

And bending down beside the glowing bars,
Murmur, a little softly, how Love fled
And paced upon the mountains over-head
And hid his face amid a crowd of stars.

—WILLIAM BUTLER YEATS

◆

Let Us Go Forth

The torch has been passed to a new generation . . .
born in this century, tempered by war, disciplined
by a hard and bitter peace, proud of our ancient
heritage—and unwilling to witness or permit the
slow undoing of those human rights to which this
nation has always been committed. . . .

With a good conscience our only sure reward,
with history the final judge of our deeds, let us go
forth to lead the land we love, asking His blessing
and His help, but knowing that here on earth God's
work must truly be our own.

—JOHN F. KENNEDY

America

O beautiful for spacious skies,
For amber waves of grain,
For purple mountain majesties
Above the fruited plain!
America! America!
God shed his grace on thee,
And crown thy good with brotherhood
From sea to shining sea!

Katharine Lee Bates

The making of an American begins at that point where he himself rejects all ties, any other history, and adopts the vesture of his adopted land.

— JAMES BALDWIN

◆

The Gift Outright

The land was ours before we were
    the land's.
She was our land more than a hundred
    years
Before we were her people. She was
    ours
In Massachusetts, in Virginia,
But we were England's, still colonials,
Possessing what we still were
    unpossessed by,
Possessed by what we now no more
    possessed.
Something we were withholding made
    us weak
Until we found out that it was ourselves
We were withholding from our land
    of living,
And forthwith found salvation in
    surrender.
Such as we were we gave ourselves
    outright
(The deed of gift was many deeds
    of war)
To the land vaguely realizing westward,
But still unstoried, artless, unenhanced,
Such as she was, such as she would
    become.

— ROBERT FROST

This generation of Americans has a rendezvous with destiny.

— FRANKLIN D. ROOSEVELT

◆

Plymouth Rock Inscription

This spot marks the final resting-place of the Pilgrims of the *Mayflower*. In weariness and hunger and in cold, fighting the wilderness and burying their dead in common graves that the Indians should not know how many had perished, they here laid the foundations of a state in which all men for countless ages should have liberty to worship God in their own way. All ye who pass by and see this stone remember, and dedicate yourselves anew to the resolution that you will not rest until this lofty ideal shall have been realized throughout the earth.

◆

Democracy is a small hard core of common agreement, surrounded by a rich variety of individual differences.

— JAMES CONANT

◆

America is not a mere body of traders; it is a body of free men. Our greatness is built upon our freedom — is moral, not material. We have a great ardor for gain; but we have a deep passion for the rights of man.

— WOODROW WILSON

Give me your tired, your poor,
Your huddled masses yearning to
  breathe free,
The wretched refuse of your teeming
  shore,
Send these, the homeless, tempest-
  tossed to me:
I lift my lamp beside the golden door.

— EMMA LAZARUS
(as inscribed on the Statue of Liberty)

♦

The history of every country begins in
the heart of a man or a woman.

— WILLA CATHER

♦

Let all the ends thou aimest at be thy
country's, thy God's and truth's. Be
noble and then nobleness that lies in
other men — sleeping but not dead —
will rise in majesty to meet thine own.

*(words carved on Union Station,
Washington, D.C.)*

♦

One Pure Source
The meaning of our word America
flows from one pure source. Within the
soul of America is the freedom of mind
and spirit in man. Here alone are the
open windows through which pours the
sunlight of all the human spirit. Here
alone human dignity is not a dream but
a major accomplishment.

— HERBERT HOOVER

Night Journey
Now as this train bears west,
Its rhythm rocks the earth,
And from my Pullman berth
I stare into the night
While others take their rest.
Bridges of iron lace,
A suddenness of trees,
A lap of mountain mist
All cross my line of sight,
Then a bleak wasted place,
And a lake below my knees.
Full on my neck I feel
The straining at a curve;
My muscles move with steel,
I wake in every nerve.
I watch a beacon swing
From dark to blazing bright;
We thunder through ravines
And gullies washèd with light.
Beyond the mountain pass
Mist deepens on the pane;
We rush into a rain
That rattles double glass.
Wheels shake the roadbed stone,
The pistons jerk and shove,
I stay up half the night
To see the land I love.

— THEODORE ROETHKE

♦

In the long view of history, these years
are the early summer of America. Our
land is young. Our strength is great.
Our course is far from run.

— LYNDON B. JOHNSON

America's Greatness

I sought for the greatness and genius of
America in her commodious harbors
and her ample rivers, and it was not
there.
I sought for the greatness and genius
of America in her fertile fields and
boundless forests, and it was not
there.
I sought for the greatness and genius of
America in her rich mines and her
vast world commerce, and it was
not there.
I sought for the greatness and genius of
America in her public school system
and her institutions of learning, and
it was not there.
I sought for the greatness and genius of
America in her democratic congress
and her matchless constitution, and
it was not there.
Not until I went into the churches of
America and heard her pulpits flame
with righteousness did I understand
the secret of her genius and power.
America is great because America is
good, and if America ever ceases
to be good, America will cease to
be great.

—ALEXIS DE TOCQUEVILLE

♦

Ask not what your country can do
for you, ask what you can do for your
country.

—JOHN F. KENNEDY

Science and time and necessity have
propelled us, the United States, to be
the general store of the world, dealers in
everything. Most of all, merchants for a
better way of life.

—LADY BIRD JOHNSON

♦

The Four Freedoms

In the future days, which we seek to
make secure, we look forward to a
world founded upon four essential
human freedoms.
The first is freedom of speech and
expression—everywhere in the
world.
The second is freedom of every person
to worship God in his own way—
everywhere in the world.
The third is freedom from want—
which, translated into world terms,
means economic understanding
which will secure to every nation a
healthy peacetime life for its inhabit-
ants—everywhere in the world.
The fourth is freedom from fear—
which, translated into world terms,
means a worldwide reduction of
armaments to such a point and in
such a fashion that no nation will
be in a position to commit an act
of physical aggression against any
neighbor—anywhere in the world.

—FRANKLIN D. ROOSEVELT

Mount Vernon Inscription

Washington, the brave, the wise, the
    good,
Supreme in war, in council, and in
    peace.
Valiant without ambition, discreet
    without fear,
Confident without presumption.
In disaster, calm; in success, moderate;
    in all, himself.
The hero, the patriot, the Christian.
The father of nations, the friend of
    mankind,
Who, when he had won all, renounced
    all,
And sought in the bosom of his family
    and of nature, retirement,
And in the hope of religion, immortality.

◆

We must have many Lincoln-hearted
men.

— VACHEL LINDSAY

◆

When an American says that he loves
his country, he means not only that he
loves the New England hills, the prairies
glistening in the sun, the wide and rising plains, the great mountains, and the
sea. He means that he loves an inner air,
an inner light in which freedom lives
and in which a man can draw the breath
of self-respect.

— ADLAI STEVENSON

What the Flag Means

The Flag is many things. It is a mark
of identification of ships at sea and of
armies in the field. It is a means of com-
munication. When you see our Flag in
front of a home, it says for all the world
to read, "Here lives a family that is
American in spirit as well as in name."
The Flag is a mirror, reflecting to each
person his own ideals and dreams. It is
a history. Its thirteen stripes and fifty
stars embrace a record written greatly
during these years since 1776. It is a
mark of pride in a great word — the
word "American." It is an aspiration of
what small children want their lives to
be. It is a memory at the end of life of
all that life has been. It is a ribbon of
honor for those who have served it
well — in peace and war. It is a warning
not to detour from the long road that
has brought our country and its people
to a degree of prosperity and happiness
never even approached under any other
banner.

— EDWARD F. HUTTON

◆

The map of America is a map of end-
lessness, of opening out, of forever and
ever. No man's face would make you
think of it but his hope might, his courage might.

— ARCHIBALD MACLEISH

Spirit of Liberty

What is the spirit of liberty? I cannot
define it; I can only tell you my own
faith. The spirit of liberty is the spirit
which is not too sure that it is right.
The spirit of liberty is the spirit which
seeks to understand the minds of other
men and women. The spirit of liberty
is the spirit which weighs their interests
alongside its own without bias. The
spirit of liberty remembers that not even
a sparrow falls to the earth unheeded.
The spirit of liberty is the spirit of Him
who, nearly two thousand years ago,
taught mankind that lesson it has never
learned, but has never quite forgotten:
that there may be a kingdom where the
least shall be heard and considered side
by side with the greatest.

◆

My Country

God grant that not only
   the love of liberty
But a thorough knowledge
   of the rights of man
May pervade all nations
   of the earth, so that
A philosopher may set
   his foot anywhere
On its surface, and say,
   "This is my country."

— BENJAMIN FRANKLIN

Break out the flag, strike up the band,
light up the sky.

— GERALD R. FORD
(national proclamation, July 1976)

◆

Our Common Labor

Before all else we seek, upon our common labor as a nation, the blessings
   of Almighty God. And the hopes
   in our hearts fashion the deepest
   prayers of our whole people.
May we pursue the right — without self-
   righteousness.
May we know unity — without confor-
   mity.
May we grow in strength — without
   pride in self.
May we, in our dealings with all peoples
   of the earth, ever speak truth and
   serve justice.
May the light of freedom, coming to all
   darkened lands, flame brightly —
   until at last the darkness is no more.
May the turbulence of our age yield to
   a true time of peace, when men and
   nations share a life that honors the
   dignity of each, the brotherhood
   of all.

— DWIGHT D. EISENHOWER

◆

The American, by nature, is optimistic.
He is experimental, an inventor and a
builder who builds best when called
upon to build greatly.

— JOHN F. KENNEDY

Aspiration

One can never consent to creep
when one feels the impulse to soar.

Helen Keller

Ah, but a man's reach should exceed
   his grasp,
Or what's a heaven for?

        — ROBERT BROWNING

♦

God the Architect
Who Thou art I know not,
   But this much I know:
Thou hast set the Pleiades
   In a silver row;

Thou hast sent the trackless winds
   Loose upon their way;
Thou hast reared a colored wall
   'Twixt the night and day;

Thou hast made the flowers to bloom
   And the stars to shine;
Hid rare gems of richest ore
   In the tunneled mine;

But chief of all thy wondrous works
   Supreme of all thy plan,
Thou hast put an upward reach
   In the heart of Man.

        — HARRY KEMP

♦

There are three ingredients in the good
life: learning, earning, and yearning.

        — CHRISTOPHER MORLEY

♦

Hitch your wagon to a star.

        — RALPH WALDO EMERSON

Some men see things as they are and say
why; I dream things that never were and
say, why not?

        — ROBERT F. KENNEDY

♦

Make no little plans; they have no
magic to stir men's blood. . . . Make big
plans, aim high in hope and work.

        — DANIEL H. BURNHAM

♦

Skylights
There are one-story intellects, two-story
intellects, and three-story intellects with
skylights. All fact collectors, who have
no aim beyond their facts, are one-story
men. Two-story men compare, reason,
generalize, using the labors of the fact
collectors as well as their own. Three-
story men idealize, imagine, predict;
their best illumination comes from
above, through the skylight.

        — OLIVER WENDELL HOLMES

♦

Reach high, for stars lie hidden in your
   soul.
Dream deep, for every dream precedes
   the goal.

        — PAMELA VAULL STARR

Ideals are like stars. You will not succeed in touching them with your hands; but, like the seafaring man, you choose them as your guides, and, following them, you will reach your destiny.

— CARL SCHURZ

Without the Way there is no going; without the Truth there is no knowing; without the Life there is no living.

— THOMAS À KEMPIS

If a man constantly aspires, is he not elevated?

— HENRY DAVID THOREAU

You Can Touch Stars
Stars have too long been symbols of the
  unattainable. They should not be
  so. For although our physical hands
  cannot reach them, we can touch
  them in other ways.
Let stars stand for those things which
  are ideal and radiant in life; if
  we seek sincerely and strive hard
  enough, it is not impossible to
  reach them, even though the goals
  seem distant at the onset.
And how often do we touch stars when
  we find them close by in the shining
  lives of great souls, in the sparkling
  universe of humanity around us!

— ESTHER BALDWIN YORK

Keep thou thy dreams — the tissue of
  all wings
  Is woven first of them; from dreams
  are made
The precious and imperishable things,
  Whose loveliness lives on, and does
  not fade

— VIRNA SHEARD

God hides some ideal in every human soul. At some time in our life we feel a trembling, fearful longing to do some good thing. Life finds its noblest spring of excellence in this hidden impulse to do our best.

— ROBERT COLLYER

It is good to have an end to journey towards; but it is the journey that matters, in the end.

— URSULA K. LE GUIN

Train your will to concentrate on a limited objective. When young you spread your effort over too many things. . . . If your try fails what does that matter — all life is a failure in the end. The thing is to get sport out of trying.

— FRANCIS CHICHESTER
(after solo sailing around the world)

Mama exhorted her children at every opportunity to "jump at de sun." We might not land on the sun, but at least we would get off the ground.

— ZORA NEALE HURSTON

♦

A Noiseless Patient Spider
A noiseless patient spider,
I mark'd where on a little promontory
   it stood isolated,
Mark'd how to explore the vacant vast
   surrounding,
It launch'd forth filament, filament,
   filament, out of itself,
Ever unreeling them, ever tirelessly
   speeding them.

And you O my soul where you stand,
Surrounded, detached, in measureless
   oceans of space,
Ceaselessly musing, venturing, throwing, seeking the spheres to connect
   them,
Till the bridge you will need be form'd,
   till the ductile anchor hold,
Till the gossamer thread you fling catch
   somewhere, O my soul.

— WALT WHITMAN

♦

Where our duty's task is wrought
In unison with God's great tho't,
The near and future blend in one,
And whatsoe'er is willed, is done.

— JOHN GREENLEAF WHITTIER

They build too low who build beneath the skies.

(inscription on a building in Washington, D.C.)

♦

The Almighty Will
The child, the seed, the grain of corn,
   The acorn on the hill,
Each for some separate end is born
   In season fit, and still
Each must in strength arise to work
   The Almighty Will.

— ROBERT LOUIS STEVENSON

♦

The most absurd and reckless aspirations have sometimes led to extraordinary success.

— VAUVENARGUES

♦

He wakes desires you never may forget;
   He shows you stars you never saw
      before;
   He makes you share with Him
      forevermore
The burden of the world's divine regret.

— ALFRED, LORD TENNYSON

♦

Only God can fully satisfy the hungry heart of man.

— HUGH BLACK

Awareness

The world will never starve
for want of wonders.

Gilbert Keith Chesterton

I saw Fair Haven Pond with its island, and meadow between the island and the shore, and a strip of perfectly still and smooth water in the lee of the island, and two hawks, fish hawks perhaps, sailing over it. I did not see how it could be improved. Yet I do not see what these things can be. I begin to see such an object when I cease to *understand* it and see that I did not realize or appreciate it before, but I get no further than this. How adapted these forms and colors to my eye! A meadow and an island! What are these things? Yet the hawks and the ducks keep so aloof! and Nature so reserved! I am made to love the pond and the meadow, as the wind is made to ripple the water.

— HENRY DAVID THOREAU

If an Arab in the desert were suddenly to discover a spring in his tent, and so would always be able to have water in abundance, how fortunate he would consider himself — so too, when a man, who as a physical being is always turned outside himself, finally turns inward and discovers that the source is within himself; not to mention his discovery that the source is his relation to God.

— SØREN KIERKEGAARD

From The Cathedral
This life were brutish did we not
   sometimes
Have intimations clear of wider scope,
Hints of occasion infinite, to keep
The soul alert with noble discontent
And onward yearnings of unstilled
   desire;
Fruitless, except we now and then
   divined
A mystery of Purpose, gleaming
   through
The secular confusions of the world,
Whose will we darkly accomplish,
   doing ours.

— JAMES RUSSELL LOWELL

It feels as if everyone who acts compassionately, works to raise consciousness, to save the planet, to make a difference in some significant way is linked to everyone else who also does. . . . Each person who follows his or her own light is a light in the web.

— JEAN SHINODA BOLEN

Infinite Space lies curved within
   the scope
Of the hand's cradle.

— EDNA ST. VINCENT MILLAY

The miracles of the church seem to me to rest not so much on faces or voices or healing power suddenly near to us from afar off, but upon our perceptions being made finer, so that for a moment our eyes can see and our ears can hear what is there about us always.

— WILLA CATHER

What else is going on right this minute while ground water creeps under my feet? The galaxy is careening in a slow, muffled widening. . . . The sun's surface is now exploding; other stars implode and vanish, heavy and black, out of sight. Meteorites are arcing to earth invisibly all day long. On the planet the winds are blowing. . . . Somewhere, someone under full sail is becalmed, in the horse latitudes, in the doldrums; in the northland, a trapper is maddened, crazed, by the eerie scent of the chinook, the snow-eater, a wind that can melt two feet of snow in a day. The pampero blows, and the tramontane, and the Boro, sirocco, levanter, mistral. Lick a finger: feel the now.

— ANNIE DILLARD

We have only this moment, sparkling like a star in our hand . . . and melting like a snowflake. Let us use it before it is too late.

— MARIE EDITH BEYNON

Two things fill me with constantly increasing admiration and awe, the longer and more earnestly I reflect on them: the starry heavens without and the moral law within.

— IMMANUEL KANT

To think of an island as a singular speck or a monument to human isolation is missing the point. Islands beget islands: a terrestrial island is surrounded by an island of water, which is surrounded by an island of air, all of which makes up our island universe. That's how the mind works too: one idea unspools into a million concentric thoughts. To sit on an island, then, is not a way of disconnecting ourselves but, rather, a way we can understand relatedness.

— GRETEL EHRLICH

The man who cannot wonder is but a pair of spectacles behind which there is no eye.

— THOMAS CARLYLE

Auguries of Innocence
To see a World in a grain of sand,
    And a Heaven in a wild flower,
Hold Infinity in the palm of your hand,
    And Eternity in an hour.

— WILLIAM BLAKE

Not By Bread Alone

Man does not live by bread alone, but by beauty and harmony, truth
and goodness, work and recreation, affection and friendship,
aspiration and worship.

Not by bread alone, but by the splendor of the firmament at night,
the glory of the heavens at dawn, the blending of colors at
sunset, the loveliness of magnolia trees, the magnificence of
mountains.

Not by bread alone, but by the majesty of ocean breakers, the
shimmer of moonlight on a calm lake, the flashing silver of a
mountain torrent, the exquisite patterns of snow crystals, the
creations of artists.

Not by bread alone, but by the sweet song of a mockingbird, the
rustle of the wind in the trees, the magic of a violin, the sublim-
ity of a softly lighted cathedral.

Not by bread alone, but by the fragrance of roses, the scent of
orange blossoms, the smell of new-mown hay, the clasp of a
friend's hand, the tenderness of a mother's kiss.

Not by bread alone, but by the lyrics of poets, the wisdom of sages,
the holiness of saints, the biographies of great souls.

Not by bread alone, but by comradeship and high adventure, seeking and finding, serving and sharing, loving and being loved.

Man does not live by bread alone, but by being faithful in prayer,
responding to the guidance of the Holy Spirit, finding and
doing the loving will of God now and eternally.

— THE UNIVERSITY PRESBYTERIAN

The Art of Awareness

Thoreau wrote: "Only that day dawns to which we are awake." The art of awareness is the art of learning how to wake up to the eternal miracle of life with its limitless possibilities.

It is rising to the challenge of the stirring old hymn: "Awake my soul, stretch every nerve."

It is developing the deep sensitivity through which you may suffer and know tragedy, and die a little, but through which you will also experience the grandeur of human life.

It is following the philosophy of Albert Schweitzer who teaches "reverence for life," from ants to men; it is developing a sense of oneness with all life.

It is identifying yourself with the hopes, dreams, fears, and longings of others, that you may understand them and help them.

It is learning to interpret the thoughts, feelings, and moods of others through their words, tones, inflections, facial expressions, and movements.

It is keeping mentally alert to all that goes on around you; it is being curious, observant, imaginative that you may build an ever increasing fund of knowledge of the universe.

It is striving to stretch the range of eye and ear; it is taking time to look and listen and comprehend.

It is searching for beauty everywhere, in a flower, a mountain, a machine, a sonnet, and a symphony.

It is knowing wonder, awe, and humility in the face of life's unexplained mysteries.

It is discovering the mystic power of the silence and coming to know the secret inner voice of intuition.

It is avoiding blind spots in considering problems and situations; it is striving "to see life steadily and see it whole."

It is enlarging the scope of your life through the expansion of your personality.

It is through a growing awareness that you stock and enrich your memory . . . and as a great philosopher has said: "A man thinks with his memory."

— WILFERD A. PETERSON

Antidote

If I had influence with the good fairy
who is supposed to preside over the
christening of all children I should ask
that her gift to each child be a sense
of wonder so indestructible that it
would last throughout life, an unfailing
antidote against the boredom and dis-
enchantment of later years, the sterile
preoccupation with things that are arti-
ficial, the alienation from the sources
of our strength.

— RACHEL CARSON

♦

Unknowingly, we plough the dust of the
stars, blown around us by the wind, and
drink the universe in a glass of rain.

— IHAB HASSAH

♦

The Mysterious

The most beautiful thing we can experience is the mysterious. It is the source
of all true art and science. He to whom
this emotion is a stranger, who can no
longer pause to wonder and stand rapt
in awe, is as good as dead: his eyes are
closed.

— ALBERT EINSTEIN

♦

To me, every hour of the day and night
is an unspeakably perfect miracle.

— WALT WHITMAN

The secret of seeing is to sail on solar
wind. Hone and spread your spirit till
you yourself are a sail, whetted, translu-
cent, broadside to the merest puff.

— ANNIE DILLARD

♦

The stuff of the world is there to be
made into images that become for us
the tabernacles of spirituality and con-
tainers of mystery. . . . The example
of artists teaches us that every day we
can transform ordinary experiences into
the material of soul — in diaries, poems,
drawings, music, letters, watercolors.

— THOMAS MOORE

♦

The delights of self-discovery are always
available.

— GAIL SHEEHY

♦

Eyes for Invisibles

I have walked with people whose eyes
are full of light but who see nothing in
sea or sky, nothing in city streets, nothing in books. It were far better to sail
forever in the night of blindness with
sense, and feeling, and mind, than to
be content with the mere act of seeing.
The only lightless dark is the night of
darkness in ignorance and insensibility.

— HELEN KELLER

A greater poverty than that caused
by lack of money is the poverty of un-
awareness. Men and women go about
the world unaware of the beauty, the
goodness, and the glories in it. Their
souls are poor. It is better to have a
poor pocketbook than to suffer from
a poor soul.

— JERRY FLEISHMAN

♦

The path zigzags up the last steepness
of the bluff and then slowly levels out.
For some distance it follows the backbone of a ridge, and then where the
ridge is narrowest there is a geat slab of
bare rock lying full in the sun. This is
what I have been looking for. I walk out
into the center of the rock and sit, the
clear warm light falling unobstructed all
around. As the sun warms me I begin
to grow comfortable not only in my
clothes, but in the place and the day.
And like those light-seeking poplars of
the ravines, my mind begins to branch
out.

— WENDELL BERRY

♦

In every age there is a turning point,
a new way of seeing and asserting the
coherence of the world.

— JACOB BRONOWSKI

Sunrise. Darkness begins to wash out
of the sky. A thick layer of fog sits in
the valley like the chrysalis of a moth.
Venus, Mercury, and Saturn burn bright
holes in the slowly bluing sky. The stars
have vanished, because by the time starlight gets to Earth it's too dim to be seen
during the daylight. Two black shapes
in the fog reel into focus as cows. A calf
reveals itself. Learning about the world
is like this — watching and waiting for
shapes to reveal themselves in the fog
of our experience.

— DIANE ACKERMAN

♦

The contrast between the bright blue
and white Christmas-tree ornament
and the black sky, that infinite universe,
and the size and significance of it really
comes through. It is so small and fragile,
such a precious little spot in that universe, that you can block it out with
your thumb. You realize that everything
that means anything to you — all of history and death and birth and love, tears
and joys, all of it, is on that little blue
and white spot out there which you can
cover with your thumb. And you realize
from that perspective that you have
changed, that there is something new,
that the relationship is no longer what
it was.

— RUSSELL SCHWEICKART

A Blessing

Just off the highway to Rochester, Minnesota,
Twilight bounds softly forth on the grass.
And the eyes of those two Indian ponies
Darken with kindness.
They have come gladly out of the willows
To welcome my friend and me.
We step over the barbed wire into the pasture
Where they have been grazing all day, alone.
They ripple tensely, they can hardly contain their
    happiness
That we have come.
They bow shyly as wet swans. They love each other.
There is no loveliness like theirs.
At home once more,
They begin munching the young tufts of spring in
    the darkness.
I would like to hold the slenderer one in my arms,
For she has walked over to me
And nuzzled my left hand.
She is black and white,
And her mane falls wild on her forehead,
And the light breeze moves me to caress her long ear
That is delicate as the skin over a girl's wrist.
Suddenly I realize
That if I stepped out of my body I would break
Into blossom.

— JAMES WRIGHT

Beauty

Beauty is God's handwriting.

Charles Kingsley

Barter

Life has loveliness to sell,
  All beautiful and splendid things,
Blue waves whitened on a cliff,
  Soaring fire that sways and sings,
And children's faces looking up
Holding wonder like a cup.

Life has loveliness to sell,
  Music like a curve of gold,
Scent of pine trees in the rain,
  Eyes that love you, arms that hold,
And for your spirit's still delight,
Holy thoughts that star the night.

Spend all you have for loveliness,
  Buy it and never count the cost;
For one white singing hour of peace
  Count many a year of strife well lost,
And for a breath of ecstasy
Give all you have been, or could be.

— SARA TEASDALE

♦

When I am working on a problem, I
never think about beauty. I only think
of how to solve the problem. But when
I have finished, if the solution is not
beautiful, I know it is wrong.

— R. BUCKMINSTER FULLER

♦

One cannot collect all the beautiful
shells on the beach.

— ANNE MORROW LINDBERGH

World Aflame

Friendships, family ties, the companionship of little children, an autumn forest
flung in prodigality against a deep blue
sky, the intricate design and haunting
fragrance of a flower, the counterpoint
of a Bach fugue or the melodic line of
a Beethoven sonata, the fluted note of
bird song, the glowing glory of a sunset:
the world is aflame with things of eternal moment.

— E. MARGARET CLARKSON

♦

Beauty is everlasting
  And dust is for a time.

— MARIANNE MOORE

♦

Loveliest of Trees

Loveliest of trees, the cherry now
Is hung with bloom along the bough,
And stands about the woodland ride
Wearing white for Eastertide.

Now, of my threescore years and ten,
Twenty will not come again,
And take from seventy springs a score,
It only leaves me fifty more.

And since to look at things in bloom
Fifty springs are little room,
About the woodlands I will go
To see the cherry hung with snow.

— A. E. HOUSMAN

Poetry

If I read a book and it makes my whole
body so cold no fire can ever warm me,
I know that is poetry. If I feel physically
as if the top of my head were taken off,
I know that is poetry. These are the only
ways I know it. Is there any other way?

— EMILY DICKINSON

◆

Night is very beautiful on this great
beach. It is the true other half of the
day's tremendous wheel; no lights
without meaning stab or trouble it;
it is beauty, it is fulfillment, it is rest.
Thin clouds float in these heavens,
islands of obscurity in a splendor of
space and stars.

— HENRY BESTON

◆

"Beauty is truth, truth beauty," — that
   is all
Ye know on earth, and all ye need to
   know.

— JOHN KEATS

◆

We ascribe beauty to that which is
simple; which has no superfluous parts;
which exactly answers its end; which
stands related to all things; which is
the mean of many extremes.

— RALPH WALDO EMERSON

Learn to foster an ardent imagination;
so shall you descry beauty which others
passed unheeded.

— NORMAN DOUGLESS

◆

New Worlds

Goethe wrote of "the Americas of the
mind." In the artist's life of the imagination there is vision and adventure and
the discovery of new worlds. An artist's
masterpiece is such an America of the
mind: a new world of meaning expressed in terms of abiding beauty, be it
in marble or paint or words or musical
tone. And in this great vision we are
privileged to share. To see eye to eye
with a great artist is to expand and
enrich the world in which we live.

— RADOSLAV A. TSANOFF

◆

Was she so loved because her eyes were
so beautiful or were her eyes so beautiful
because she was so loved?

— ANZIA YEZIERSKA

◆

God scatters beauty as he scatters
   flowers
O'er the wide earth, and tells us all
   are ours.
A hundred lights in every temple burn,
And at each shrine I bend my knee
   in turn.

— WALTER SAVAGE LANDOR

Too Little Time

I still find each day too short for all the
thoughts I want to think, all the walks
I want to take, all the books I want to
read, and all the friends I want to see.
The longer I live the more my mind
dwells upon the beauty and the wonder
of the world.

— JOHN BURROUGHS

◆

God's World

O World, I cannot hold thee close
   enough!
  Thy winds, thy wide grey skies!
  Thy mists that roll and rise!
Thy woods, this autumn day, that ache
   and sag
And all but cry with colour! That
   gaunt crag
To crush! To lift the lean of that black
   bluff!
World, World, I cannot get thee close
   enough!
Long have I known a glory in it all,
  But never knew I this;
  Here such a passion is
As stretcheth me apart. Lord, I do fear
Thou'st made the world too beautiful
   this year,
My soul is all but out of me—let fall
No burning leaf; prithee, let no bird
   call.

— EDNA ST. VINCENT MILLAY

Beauty is the only thing that time cannot harm. Philosophies fall away like
sand, and creeds follow one another
like the withered leaves of Autumn; but
what is beautiful is a joy for all seasons
and a possession for all eternity.

— OSCAR WILDE

◆

Miracle

Who is in love with loveliness,
  Need not shake with cold;
For he may tear a star in two,
  And frock himself in gold.

Who holds her first within his heart,
  In certain favor goes;
If his roof tumbles, he may find
  Harbor in a rose.

— LIZETTE WOODWORTH REESE

◆

Beauty of whatever kind, in its supreme
development, invariably excites the
sensitive soul to tears.

— EDGAR ALLAN POE

◆

A thing of beauty is a joy forever:
Its loveliness increases; it will never
Pass into nothingness; but still will keep
A bower quiet for us, and a sleep
Full of sweet dreams, and health, and
   quiet breathing.

— JOHN KEATS

Character

It is not what he has, nor even what
he does, which directly expresses the worth
of a man, but what he is.

Henri Frederic Amiel

I will hew great windows, wonderful
windows, measureless windows for my
soul.

—ANGELA MORGAN

Be the Best of Whatever You Are
If you can't be a pine on the top of
   the hill,
   Be a scrub in the valley—but be
The best little scrub by the side of
   the rill;
   Be a bush if you can't be a tree.

If you can't be a bush, be a bit of
   the grass,
   Some highway happier make;
If you can't be a muskie, then just be
   a bass—
   But the liveliest bass in the lake!

We can't all be captains, we've got to
   be crew,
   There's something for all of us here,
There's big work to do, and there's lesser
   to do,
   And the task we must do is the near.

If you can't be a highway, then just be
   a trail,
   If you can't be the sun, be a star;
It isn't by size that you win or you fail—
   Be the best of whatever you are!

—DOUGLAS MALLOCH

Character is what you are in the dark.

—DWIGHT L. MOODY

Good habits are not made on birthdays,
nor Christian character at the new year.
The workshop of character is everyday
life. The uneventful and commonplace
hour is where the battle is lost or won.

—MALTBIE D. BABCOCK

Never bend your head. Always hold
it high. Look the world straight in
the face.

—HELEN KELLER
(to a five-year-old blind child)

Splendid Gift
Live your life while you have it. Life is
a splendid gift. There is nothing small
in it. For the greatest things grow by
God's Law out of the smallest. But to
live your life you must discipline it. You
must not fritter it away in "fair purpose,
erring act, inconstant will" but make
your thoughts, your acts, all work to
the same end and that end, not self but
God. That is what we call character.

—FLORENCE NIGHTINGALE

The best index to a person's character
is (a) how he treats people who can't
do him any good, and (b) how he treats
people who can't fight back.

—ABIGAIL VAN BUREN

You should remember that though another may have more money, beauty, and brains than you, yet when it comes to the rarer spiritual values such as charity, self-sacrifice, honor, nobility of heart, you have an equal chance with everyone to be the most beloved and honored of all people.

— ARCHIBALD RUTLEDGE

♦

Character is much more easily kept than recovered.

♦

The quality of strength lined with tenderness is an unbeatable combination, as are intelligence and necessity when unblunted by formal education.

— MAYA ANGELOU

♦

He that walketh with wise men shall be wise: but a companion of fools shall be destroyed.

— PROVERBS 13:20

♦

Spiritual maturity begins when we realize that we are God's guests in this world. We are not householders, but pilgrims; not landlords, but tenants; not owners, but guests.

— C. WILLARD FETTER

This above all: to thine own self be true, And it must follow, as the night the day, Thou canst not then be false to any man.

— WILLIAM SHAKESPEARE

♦

The finest qualities of our characters do not come from trying but from that mysterious and yet most effective capacity to be inspired.

— HARRY EMERSON FOSDICK

♦

I think character never changes; the Acorn becomes an Oak, which is very little like an Acorn to be sure, but it never becomes an Ash.

— HESTER LYNCH PIOZZI

♦

Not often in the story of mankind does a man arrive on earth who is both steel and velvet, who is hard as rock and soft as drifting fog, who holds in his heart and mind the paradox of terrible storm and peace unspeakable and perfect.

— CARL SANDBURG
(addressing the joint session of Congress marking the 150th anniversary of Lincoln's birth)

♦

If a man is not faithful to his own individuality, he cannot be loyal to anything.

— CLAUDE MCKAY

Reputation is what men and women think of us; character is what God and the angels know of us.

— THOMAS PAINE

◆

Sow a thought, and you reap an act;
Sow an act, and you reap a habit;
Sow a habit and you reap a character;
Sow a character and you reap a destiny.

◆

You can construct the character of a man and his age not only from what he does and says, but from what he fails to say and do.

— NORMAN DOUGLAS

◆

The tissue of the Life to be
    We weave with colors all our own,
And in the field of Destiny
    We reap as we have sown.

— JOHN GREENLEAF WHITTIER

◆

It is more important to understand the ground of your own behavior than to understand the motives of another.

— DAG HAMMARSKJÖLD

◆

Unless I accept my faults I will most certainly doubt my virtues.

— HUGH PRATHER

Men would like to love themselves, but they usually find that they cannot. That is because they have built an ideal image of themselves which puts their real self in the shade.

— GERALD BRENAN

◆

Character, not circumstances, make the man.

— BOOKER T. WASHINGTON

◆

Better keep yourself clean and bright; you are the window through which you must see the world.

— GEORGE BERNARD SHAW

◆

Lincoln

There is no new thing to be said of Lincoln. There is no new thing to be said of the mountains, or of the sea, or of the stars. The years may go their way, but the same old mountains lift their granite shoulders above the drifting clouds, the same mysterious seas beat upon the shore, and the same silent stars keep holy vigil above a tired world. But to mountains and seas and stars men turn forever in unwearied homage. And thus with Lincoln. For he was mountain in grandeur of soul; he was sea in deep undervoice of mystic loneliness; he was star in steadfast purity of purpose and of service. And he abides.

— HOMER HOCK

The tragedy of the world is that men have given first class loyalty to second class causes and these causes have betrayed them.

— LYNN HAROLD HOUGH

♦

Glass, china, and reputation are easily cracked and never well mended.

— BENJAMIN FRANKLIN

♦

The measure of a man's real character is what he would do if he knew he would never be found out.

— THOMAS BABINGTON MACAULAY

♦

Thank God that I can trust,
That tho' a thousand times I feel
   the thrust
Of Faith betrayed, I still have faith
   in man,
Believe him pure and good since
   time began,
Thy child forever, tho' he may forget
The perfect mold in which his soul
   was set.

— ANGELA MORGAN

♦

A half century of living should put a good deal into a woman's face besides a few wrinkles and some unwelcome folds around the chin.

— FRANCES PARKINSON KEYES

A good name is rather to be chosen than great riches, and loving favor rather than silver and gold.

— PROVERBS 22:1

♦

Why should we be in such desperate haste to succeed and in such desperate enterprises? If a man does not keep pace with his companions, perhaps it is because he hears a different drummer. Let him step to the music which he hears, however measured or far off. It is not important that he should mature as soon as an apple tree or an oak. Shall he turn his spring into summer?

— HENRY DAVID THOREAU

♦

Nearly all men can stand adversity, but if you want to test a man's character, give him power.

— ABRAHAM LINCOLN

♦

It would not be easy, even now, even for an unbeliever, to find a better translation of virtue from the abstract into the concrete than so to live that Christ would approve his life.

— JOHN STUART MILL

♦

Every man has three characters—that which he exhibits, that which he has, and that which he thinks he has.

— ALPHONSE KERR

Reputation and Character

The circumstances amid which you live determine your
reputation; the truth you believe determines your
character.

Reputation is what you are supposed to be; character is
what you are.

Reputation is the photograph; character is the face.

Reputation comes over one from without; character grows
up from within.

Reputation is what you have when you come to a new
community; character is what you have when you
go away.

Your reputation is learned in an hour; your character does
not come to light for a year.

Reputation is made in a moment; character is built in a
lifetime.

Reputation grows like a mushroom; character grows like
the oak.

A single newspaper report gives you your reputation; a life
of toil gives you your character.

Reputation makes you rich or makes you poor; character
makes you happy or makes you miserable.

Reputation is what men say about you on your tombstone;
character is what angels say about you before the
throne of God.

— WILLIAM HERSEY DAVIS

Children

Every child comes with the message
that God is not yet discouraged of man.

Rabindranath Tagore

Life is a flame that is always burning
itself out, but it catches fire again every
time a child is born.

— GEORGE BERNARD SHAW

You may give them your love but not
  your thoughts,
For they have their own thoughts.
You may house their bodies but not
  their souls,
For their souls dwell in the house of
  tomorrow, which you cannot visit,
  not even in your dreams.
You may strive to be like them, but
  seek not to make them like you.
For life goes not backward nor tarries
  with yesterday.
You are the bows from which your children as living arrows are sent forth.

— KAHLIL GIBRAN

God's Opinion

A baby is God's opinion that life should
go on. Never will a time come when
the most marvelous recent invention
is as marvelous as a newborn baby.
The finest of our precision watches, the
most supercolossal of our supercargo
planes, don't compare with a newborn
baby in the number and ingenuity
of coils and springs, in the flow and
change of chemical solutions, in timing
devices and interrelated parts that are
irreplaceable.

— CARL SANDBURG

Two Prayers

Last night my little boy confessed
    to me
Some childish wrong;
And kneeling at my knee,
He prayed with tears —
"Dear God, make me a man
Like Daddy — wise and strong;
I know you can."

Then while he slept
I knelt beside his bed,
Confessed my sins,
And prayed with low-bowed head —
"O God, make me a child
Like my child here —
Pure, guileless,
Trusting Thee with faith sincere."

— ANDREW GILLIES

A newborn baby is an extraordinary
event, and I have never seen two babies
who looked exactly alike. Here is the
breathing miracle who could not live an
instant without you, with a skull more
fragile than an egg, a miracle of eyes,
legs, toenails, and lungs.

— JAMES BALDWIN

I must take issue with the term "a mere
child," for it has been my invariable experience that the company of a mere
child is infinitely preferable to that of
a mere adult.

— FRAN LEBOWITZ

Making the decision to have a child—
it's momentous. It is to decide forever
to have your heart walking outside your
body.

— ELIZABETH STONE

♦

The Heart of a Child

Our religion is one which challenges
the ordinary human standards by holding that the ideal of life is the spirit of
a little child. We tend to glorify adult-
hood and wisdom and worldly pru-
dence, but the Gospel reverses all this.
The Gospel says that the inescapable
condition of entrance into the divine
fellowship is that we turn and become
as a little child. As against our natural
judgment we must become tender and
full of wonder and unspoiled by the
hard skepticism on which we so often
pride ourselves. But when we really look
into the heart of a child, willful as he
may be, we are often ashamed. God has
sent children into the world, not only
to replenish it, but to serve as sacred
reminders of something ineffably precious which we are always in danger of
losing. The sacrament of childhood is
thus a continuing revelation.

— ELTON TRUEBLOOD

♦

Children have never been very good at
listening to their elders, but they have
never failed to imitate them.

— JAMES BALDWIN

Even a child is known by his doings,
whether his work be pure, and whether
it be right.

— PROVERBS 20:11

♦

We need love's tender lessons taught
  As only weakness can;
God hath his small interpreters;
  The child must teach the man.

— JOHN GREENLEAF WHITTIER

♦

The time and the quality of the time
that their parents devote to them indi-
cate to children the degree to which
they are valued by their parents. . . .
When children know that they are valued, when they truly feel valued in the
deepest parts of themselves, then they
feel valuable. This knowledge is worth
more than any gold.

— M. SCOTT PECK

♦

Whoever inquires about our childhood
wants to know something about our
soul.

— ERIKA BURKHART

♦

Words are more powerful than perhaps
anyone suspects, and once deeply en-
graved in a child's mind, they are not
easily eradicated.

— MAY SARTON

Children

What Is a Girl?

Little girls are the nicest things that happen to people. They are born with a little bit of angelshine about them, and though it wears thin sometimes, there is always enough left to lasso your heart — even when they are sitting in the mud, or crying temperamental tears, or parading up the street in Mother's best clothes.

A little girl can be sweeter (and badder) oftener than anyone else in the world. She can jitter around, and stomp, and make funny noises that frazzle your nerves, yet just when you open your mouth, she stands there demure with that special look in her eyes. A girl is Innocence playing in the mud, Beauty standing on its head, and Motherhood dragging a doll by the foot. . . .

God borrows from many creatures to make a little girl. He uses the song of a bird, the squeal of a pig, the stubbornness of a mule, the antics of a monkey, the spryness of a grasshopper, the curiosity of a cat, the speed of a gazelle, the slyness of a fox, the softness of a kitten, and to top it all off He adds the mysterious mind of a woman.

A little girl likes new shoes, party dresses, small animals, first grade, noisemakers, the girl next door, dolls, make-believe, dancing lessons, ice cream, kitchens, coloring books, make-up, cans of water, going visiting, tea parties, and one boy. She doesn't care so much for visitors, boys in general, large dogs, hand-me-downs, straight chairs, vegetables, snowsuits, or staying in the front yard. She is loudest when you are thinking, the prettiest when she has provoked you, the busiest at bedtime, the quietest when you want to show her off, and the most flirtatious when she absolutely must not get the best of you again.

Who else can cause you more grief, joy, irritation, satisfaction, embarrassment, and genuine delight than this combination of Eve, Salome, and Florence Nightingale? She can muss up your home, your hair, and your dignity — spend your money, your time, and your patience — and just when your temper is ready to crack, her sunshine peeks through and you've lost again.

Yes, she is a nerve-racking nuisance, just a noisy bundle of mischief. But when your dreams tumble down and the world is a mess — when it seems you are pretty much of a fool after all — she can make you a king when she climbs on your knee and whispers, "I love you best of all!"

— ALAN BECK

Children

What Is a Boy?

Between the innocence of babyhood and the dignity of manhood we find a delightful creature called a boy. Boys come in assorted sizes, weights, and colors, but all boys have the same creed: to enjoy every second of every minute of every hour of every day and to protest with noise (their only weapon) when their last minute is finished and the adult males pack them off to bed at night.

Boys are found everywhere—on top of, underneath, inside of, climbing on, swinging from, running around, or jumping to. Mothers love them, little girls hate them, older sisters and brothers tolerate them, adults ignore them, and Heaven protects them. A boy is Truth with dirt on its face, Beauty with a cut on its finger, Wisdom with bubble gum in its hair, and the Hope of the future with a frog in its pocket.

When you are busy, a boy is an inconsiderate, bothersome, intruding jangle of noise. When you want him to make a good impression, his brain turns to jelly or else he becomes a savage, sadistic, jungle creature bent on destroying the world and himself with it.

A boy is a composite—he has the appetite of a horse, the digestion of a sword swallower, the energy of a pocket-sized atomic bomb, the curiosity of a cat, the lungs of a dictator, the imagination of a Paul Bunyan, the shyness of a violet, the audacity of a steel trap, the enthusiasm of a firecracker, and when he makes something he has five thumbs on each hand.

He likes ice cream, knives, saws, Christmas, comic books, the boy across the street, woods, water (in its natural habitat), large animals, Dad, trains, Saturday mornings, and fire engines. He is not much for Sunday School, company, schools, books without pictures, music lessons, neckties, barbers, girls, overcoats, adults, or bedtime.

Nobody else is so early to rise, or so late to supper. Nobody else gets so much fun out of trees, dogs, and breezes. Nobody else can cram into one pocket a rusty knife, a half-eaten apple, three feet of string, an empty Bull Durham sack, two gum drops, six cents, a slingshot, a chunk of unknown substance, and a genuine supersonic code ring with a secret compartment.

A boy is a magical creature—you can lock him out of your workshop, but you can't lock him out of your heart. You can get him out of your study, but you can't get him out of your mind. Might as well give up—he is your captor, your jailor, your boss, and your master—a freckled-faced, pint-sized, cat-chasing, bundle of noise. But when you come home at night with only the shattered pieces of your hopes and dreams, he can mend them like new with the two magic words, "Hi Dad!"

—ALAN BECK

If...

If a child lives with criticism, he learns
to condemn.

If a child lives with hostility, he learns
to fight.

If a child lives with fears, he learns to
be apprehensive.

If a child lives with pity, he learns to feel
sorry for himself.

If a child lives with jealousy, he learns to
feel guilty.

If a child lives with encouragement, he
learns to be confident.

If a child lives with tolerance, he learns
to be patient.

If a child lives with praise, he learns to
be appreciative.

If a child lives with acceptance, he learns
to love.

If a child lives with approval, he learns
to like himself.

If a child lives with recognition, he
learns to have a goal.

If a child lives with fairness, he learns
what justice is.

If a child lives with honesty, he learns
what truth is.

If a child lives with security, he learns
to have faith in himself and in those
about him.

If a child lives with friendliness, he
learns that the world is a good place
in which to live.

— THE WATCHMAN-EXAMINER

There is just one way to bring up a
child in the way he should go, and that
is to travel that way yourself.

— ABRAHAM LINCOLN

What the majority of American children needs is to stop being pampered,
stop being indulged, stop being chauf-
fered, stop being catered to. In the final
analysis, it is not what you do for your
children but what you have taught them
to do for themselves that will make
them successful human beings.

— ANN LANDERS

When they tell you to grow up, they
mean stop growing.

— TOM ROBBINS

I believe the power of observation in
numbers of very young children to be
quite wonderful for its closeness and
accuracy. Indeed, I think that most
grown men who are remarkable in this
respect, may with greater propriety be
said not to have lost the faculty, than to
have acquired it; the rather, as I generally observe such men to retain a certain
freshness, and gentleness, and capacity
of being pleased, which are also an in-
heritance they have preserved from their
childhood.

— CHARLES DICKENS

Community

Outwitted

He drew a circle that shut me out—
Heretic, rebel, a thing to flout.
But Love and I had the wit to win;
We drew a circle that took him in!

Edwin Markham

What Is Brotherhood?

What is brotherhood? It is the wisdom
of Lincoln and the warmth of Gandhi.
It is the humility of Jesus, the humbleness of Mohammed, and the humani-
tarianism of Confucius. It is Catholic
and Protestant and Jew living together
in peacefulness and harmony. It is Italian and Dane and Bulgarian and Pole
working side by side on the job and sitting shoulder to shoulder in the union
hall searching for ways to advance the
common good. It is the Ten Commandments and the Sermon on the Mount.
It is the Bible, the Talmud, and the Ko-
ran. It is the essence of all wisdom of
all the ages distilled into a single word.
But equally it is the understanding of
neighbors and friends who sorrow at
your misfortunes and rejoice at your
triumphs. You cannot see brotherhood;
neither can you hear it nor taste it. But
you can feel it a hundred times a day.
It is the pat on the back when things
look gloomy. It is the smile of encouragement when the way seems hard. It
is the helping hand when the burden
becomes unbearable.

— PETER E. TERZICK

♦

Have Love. Not love alone for one,
 But man as man thy brother call;
And scatter like the circling sun
 Thy charities on all.

— JOHANN VON SCHILLER

The greatest challenge of the day is:
how to bring about a revolution of the
heart, a revolution which has to start
with each one of us? When we begin to
take the lowest places, to wash the feet
of others, to love our brothers with that
burning love, that passion, which led to
the Cross, then we can truly say, "Now
I have begun."

— DOROTHY DAY

♦

I sought my soul,
 But my soul I could not see.
I sought my God,
 But my God eluded me.
I sought my brother,
 And I found all three.

♦

Morality is always higher than laws and
we cannot forget this ever.

— ALEKSANDR SOLZHENITSYN

♦

Very seldom will a person give up on
himself. He continues to have hope
because he knows he has the potential
for change. He tries again—not just to
exist, but to bring about those changes
in himself that will make his life worth
living. Yet people are very quick to give
up on friends, and especially on their
spouses, to declare them hopeless, and
to either walk away or do nothing
more than resign themselves to a bad
situation.

— HUGH PRATHER

Let us be kinder to one another.

— ALDOUS HUXLEY
(his last words)

◆

Only when one is connected to one's own core is one connected to others.

— ANNE MORROW LINDBERGH

◆

A *Creed*

There is a destiny that makes us
   brothers;
  None goes his way alone:
All that we send into the lives of others
  Comes back into our own.
I care not what his temples or his creeds,
  One thing holds firm and fast —
That into his fateful heap of days and
  deeds
  The soul of man is cast.

— EDWIN MARKHAM

◆

Grant us brotherhood, not only for this day but for all our years — a brotherhood not of words but of acts and deeds.

— STEPHEN VINCENT BENÉT

◆

Then let us pray that come it may, —
As come it will for a' that, —
That man to man, the world o'er,
Shall brothers be for a' that.

— ROBERT BURNS

Prayer

Give us, Lord, a bit o' sun,
A bit o' work, and a bit o' fun;
Give us all in the struggle and splutter,
Our daily bread and a bit o' butter.

Give us, Lord, a chance to be
Our goodly best, brave, wise, and free,
Our goodly best for ourselves and
   others,
Till all men learn to live as brothers.

(from an old English inn)

◆

If civilization is to survive, we must cultivate the science of human relationships — the ability of all peoples, of all kinds, to live together, in the same world at peace.

— FRANKLIN D. ROOSEVELT

◆

To love deeply in one direction makes us more loving in all others.

— ANNE-SOPHIE SWETCHINE

◆

Blessed is the servant who loves his brother as much when he is sick and useless as when he is well and can be of service to him. And blessed is he who loves his brother as well when he is afar off as when he is by his side, and who would say nothing behind his back he might not, in love, say before his face.

— ST. FRANCIS OF ASSISI

It is a serious thing to live in a society of possible gods and goddesses, to remember that the dullest and most uninteresting person you can talk to may one day be a creature which, if you saw it now, you would be strongly tempted to worship, or else a horror and corruption such as you now meet, if at all, only in nightmare. All day long we are, in some degree, helping each other to one or the other of these destinations. It is in the light of these overwhelming possibilities, it is in the awe and circumspection proper to them that we should conduct all our dealings with one another, all friendships, all loves, all play, all politics. There are no *ordinary* people. You have never talked to a mere mortal.

— C. S. LEWIS

♦

A great many people think they are thinking when they are merely rearranging their prejudices.

— WILLIAM JAMES

♦

To have courage without pugnacity,
to have conviction without bigotry,
to have charity without condescension,
to have faith without credulity,
to have love of humanity without
    mere sentimentality,
to have meekness with power
and emotion with sanity —
that is brotherhood.

— CHARLES EVANS HUGHES

For Whom the Bell Tolls
No man is an island entire of itself. Every man is a piece of the continent, a part of the main. If a clod be washed away by the sea, Europe is the less, as well as if a promontory were, as well as if a manor of thy friends or of thine own were. Any man's death diminishes me, because I am involved in mankind. Therefore never send to know for whom the bell tolls. It tolls for thee.

— JOHN DONNE

♦

We cannot live only for ourselves. A thousand fibers connect us with our fellow men; and among those fibers, as sympathetic threads, our actions run as causes, and they come back to us as effects.

— HERMAN MELVILLE

♦

A wonderful fact to reflect upon, that every human creature is constituted to be that profound secret and mystery to every other. A solemn consideration, when I enter a great city by night, that every one of those darkly clustered houses encloses its own secret; that every room in every one of them encloses its own secret; that every beating heart in the thousands of breasts there is, in some of its imaginings, a secret to the heart nearest it.

— CHARLES DICKENS

Confidence

I can see how it might be possible
for a man to look down upon the earth
and be an atheist, but I cannot conceive
how he could look up into the heavens
and say there is no God.

Abraham Lincoln

But those who hope in the Lord
    will renew their strength.
They will soar on wings like eagles;
    they will run and not grow weary,
    they will walk and not be faint.

—ISAIAH 40:31

Undergirding

Faith is a living, daring confidence in God's grace, so sure and certain that a man would stake his life on it a thousand times. This confidence in God's grace and knowledge of it makes men glad and bold and happy in dealing with God and with all his creatures; and this is the work of the Holy Ghost in faith. Hence a man is ready and glad, without compulsion, to do good to everyone, to serve everyone, to suffer everything, in love and praise of God, who has shown him this grace.

—MARTIN LUTHER

Tell him about the heartache,
And tell him the longings, too.
Tell him the baffled purpose
When we scarce know what to do.

Then leaving all our weakness
With the One divinely strong,
Forget that we bore a burden
And carry away a song.

—PHILLIPS BROOKS

Every great discovery I ever made, I gambled that the truth was there, and then I acted on it in faith until I could prove its existence.

—ARTHUR H. COMPTON

Let nothing disturb thee,
Nothing affright thee;
All things are passing;
God never changeth;
Patient endurance
Attaineth to all things.
Whom God possesseth
In nothing is wanting:
Alone God sufficeth.

—ST. TERESA

I'll walk where my own nature would
    be leading—
It vexes me to choose another guide.

—EMILY BRONTË

If you doubt you can accomplish something, then you can't accomplish it. You have to have confidence in your ability, and then be tough enough to follow through.

—ROSALYNN CARTER

I believe that in our constant search for security we can never gain any peace of mind until we secure our own soul. And this I do believe above all, especially in my times of greatest discouragement, *that I must believe*—that I must believe in my fellow man—that I must believe in myself—that I must believe in God— if life is to have any meaning.

—MARGARET CHASE SMITH

◆

Trust your hunches. They're usually based on facts filed away just below your conscious level.

—JOYCE BROTHERS

◆

I see the rainbow in the sky, the
   dew upon the grass;
I see them, and I ask not why they
   glimmer or they pass.
With folded arms I linger not to
   call them back; 'twere vain:
In this, or in some other spot, I
   know they'll shine again.

—WALTER SAVAGE LANDOR

◆

If there is a faith that can move mountains, it is faith in your own power.

—MARIE VON EBNER-ESCHENBACH

Our belief at the beginning of a doubtful undertaking is the one thing that insures the successful outcome of our venture.

—WILLIAM JAMES

◆

Overtones

I heard a bird at break of day
   Sing from the autumn trees
A song so mystical and calm,
   So full of certainties,
No man, I think, could listen long
   Except upon his knees.
Yet this was but a simple bird,
   Alone, among the trees.

—WILLIAM ALEXANDER PERCY

◆

Confidence . . . thrives on honesty, on honor, on the sacredness of obligations, on faithful protection and on unselfish performance. Without them it cannot live.

—FRANKLIN D. ROOSEVELT

◆

I believe in God, in the same way in which I believe in my friends, because I feel the breath of his love and his invisible, intangible hand, bringing me here, carrying me there, pressing upon me.

—MIGUEL DE UNAMUNO

Kill the snake of doubt in your soul,
crush the worms of fear in your heart
and mountains will move out of your
way.

— KATE SEREDY

♦

They are able because they think they
are able.

— VIRGIL

♦

The Cross

Because the cross alone measures "the
breadth, and length, and depth, and
height" of the love of God, it is beyond
the comprehension of man. The love
of Christ "passeth knowledge." Its
"breadth" is wide enough to comprehend the whole world, including all
races. Its "length" reaches down through
all the ages from the beginning to the
end of the reign of sin. Its "depth"
reaches down to the lowest deeps of
man's degradation and saves even "to
the uttermost." Its "height" includes
the highest heaven to which it will
eventually lift those who know its
power.

— TAYLOR G. BUNCH

♦

Believe that life is worth living, and
your belief will help create the fact.

— WILLIAM JAMES

He paints the lily of the field,
 Perfumes each lily bell;
If he so loves the little flowers,
 I know he loves me well.

— MARIA STRAUS

♦

Be like the bird, pausing in his flight
On limb too slight,
Feels it give way, yet sings,
Knowing he has wings.

— VICTOR HUGO

♦

Underlying the whole scheme of civilization is the confidence men have in
each other, confidence in their integrity,
confidence in their honesty, confidence
in their future.

— W. BOURKE COCKRAN

♦

If one burdens the future with one's
worries, it cannot grow organically. I am
filled with confidence, not that I shall
succeed in worldly things, but that even
when things go badly for me I shall still
find life good and worth living.

— ETTY HILLESUM

♦

The confidence which we have in ourselves gives birth to much of that which
we have in others.

— LA ROCHEFOUCAULD

Courage

Courage is the first of human
qualities because it is the quality
which guarantees all the others.

Winston Churchill

When you get in a tight place and everything goes against you, till it seems you could not hold on a minute longer, never give up then, for that is just the place and time that the tide will turn.

— HARRIET BEECHER STOWE

♦

Keep your fears to yourself, but share your courage with others.

— ROBERT LOUIS STEVENSON

♦

Courage is the price
that life extracts
for granting peace.
The soul
that knows it not,
knows no release
from little things.

— AMELIA EARHART

♦

The hero is no braver than an ordinary man, but he is brave five minutes longer.

— RALPH WALDO EMERSON

♦

I wanted you to see what real courage is, instead of getting the idea that courage is a man with a gun in his hand. It's when you know you're licked before you begin but you begin anyway and you see it through no matter what.

— HARPER LEE

To fight aloud is very brave,
But gallanter, I know,
Who charge within the bosom
The cavalry of woe.

— EMILY DICKINSON

♦

To defend one's self against fear is simply to insure that one will, one day, be conquered by it; fears must be faced.

— JAMES BALDWIN

♦

Profile in Courage
To be courageous requires no exceptional qualifications, no magic formula, no special combination of time, place, and circumstance. It is an opportunity that sooner or later is presented to us all. Politics merely furnish one arena which imposes special tests of courage. In whatever arena of life one may meet the challenge of courage, whatever may be the sacrifices he faces if he follows his conscience — the loss of his friends, his fortune, his contentment, even the esteem of his fellow men — each man must decide for himself the course he will follow. The stories of past courage can define that ingredient — they can teach, they can offer hope, they can provide inspiration. But they cannot supply courage itself. For this each man must look into his own soul.

— JOHN F. KENNEDY

Courage and clemency are equal virtues.

— MARY DELARIVIER MANLEY

◆

Dikes of Courage

Courage and cowardice are antithetical.
Courage is an inner resolution to go
    forward in spite of obstacles and
    frightening situations; cowardice is
    a submissive surrender to circum-
    stance.
Courage breeds creative self-affirmation;
    cowardice produces destructive self-
    abnegation.
Courage faces fear and thereby masters
    it; cowardice represses fear and is
    thereby mastered by it.
Courageous men never lose the zest for
    living even though their life situa-
    tion is zestless; cowardly men, over-
    whelmed by the uncertainties of life
    lose the will to live.
We must constantly build dikes of cour-
    age to hold back the flood of fear.

— MARTIN LUTHER KING, JR.

◆

The world has no room for cowards, We
must all be ready somehow to toil, to
suffer, to die. And yours is not the less
noble because no drum beats before you
when you go out to your daily battle-
fields, and no crowds shout your coming
when you return from your daily victory
and defeat.

— ROBERT LOUIS STEVENSON

Prayer

I do not ask to walk smooth paths
Nor bear an easy load.
I pray for strength and fortitude
To climb the rock-strewn road.

Give me such courage I can scale
The hardest peaks alone,
And transform every stumbling block
Into a steppingstone.

— GAIL BROOK BURKET

◆

Courage is what it takes to stand up and
speak; courage is also what it takes to sit
down and listen.

◆

One has to abandon altogether the
search for security, and reach out to the
risk of living with both arms. One has
to embrace the world like a lover. One
has to accept pain as a condition of
existence. One has to court doubt and
darkness as the cost of knowing. One
needs a will stubborn in conflict, but
apt always to total acceptance of every
consequence of living and dying.

— MORRIS L. WEST

◆

Why not go out on a limb? Isn't that
where the fruit is?

— FRANK SCULLY

Courage is resistance to fear, not absence of it.

— MARK TWAIN

The courage of life is often a less dramatic spectacle than the courage of a final moment; but it is no less than a magnificent mixture of triumph and tragedy. A man does what he must — in spite of personal consequences, in spite of obstacles and dangers and pressures — and that is the basis of all human morality.

— JOHN F. KENNEDY

Courage conquers all things.

— OVID

Last, but by no means least, courage — moral courage, the courage of one's convictions, the courage to see things through. The world is in a constant conspiracy against the brave. It's the age-old struggle — the roar of the crowd on one side and the voice of your conscience on the other.

— DOUGLAS MACARTHUR

It is better to live one day as a lion than a hundred years as a sheep.

— ITALIAN MOTTO

Bravery is not an individual, a racial, a national quality, in which some excel others per se. It is an accident of circumstances.

— MICHAEL J. DEE

Valor lies just half-way between rashness and cowardice.

— CERVANTES

I looked more widely around me, I studied the lives of the masses of humanity, and I saw that, not two or three, or ten, but hundreds, thousands, millions, had so understood the meaning of life that they were able both to live and to die. All these men were well acquainted with the meaning of life and death, quietly labored, endured privation and suffering, lived and died, and saw in all this, not a vain, but a good thing.

— LEO TOLSTOY

Perfect courage is to do unwitnessed what we should be capable of doing before all the world.

— LA ROCHEFOUCAULD

True courage is not only a balloon for rising but also a parachute for falling.

— LUDWIG BÖRNE

Criticism

The question is not what a man
can scorn, or disparage, or find fault with,
but what he can love, and value,
and appreciate.

John Ruskin

You do ill if you praise, but worse if you censure, what you do not rightly understand.

— LEONARDO DA VINCI

No one can make you feel inferior without your consent.

— ELEANOR ROOSEVELT

Three Gates
If you are tempted to reveal
A tale to you someone has told
About another, make it pass,
Before you speak, three gates of gold.
These narrow gates: First, "Is it true?"
Then, "Is it needful?" In your mind
Give truthful answer. And the next
Is last and narrowest, "Is it kind?"
And if to reach your lips at last
It passes through these gateways three,
Then you may tell the tale, nor fear
What the result of speech may be.

— FROM THE ARABIAN

It is much easier to be critical than correct.

— BENJAMIN DISRAELI

No matter how much you disagree with your kin, if you are a thoroughbred you will not discuss their shortcomings with the neighbors.

— TOM THOMPSON

To speak ill of others is a dishonest way of praising ourselves; let us be above such transparent egotism. . . . If you can't say good and encouraging things, say nothing. Nothing is often a good thing to say, and always a clever thing to say.

— WILL DURANT

He who cannot forgive breaks the bridge over which he himself must pass.

— GEORGE HERBERT

Critics
What one approves, another scorns,
And thus his nature each discloses;
You find the rosebush full of thorns,
I find the thornbush full of roses.

— ARTHUR GUITERMAN

Speak ill of no man, but speak all the good you know of everybody.

— BENJAMIN FRANKLIN

A fly may sting a stately horse and make him wince, but one is but an insect, and the other is a horse still.

— SAMUEL JOHNSON

Be not angry that you cannot make others as you wish them to be, since you cannot make yourself as you wish to be.

— THOMAS À KEMPIS

Sunrises and Cyclones

It seems to be a general belief that the will of God is to make things distasteful for us, like taking bad-tasting medicine when we are sick, or going to the dentist. Somebody needs to tell us that sunrise is also God's will. There is the time of harvest, the harvest which will provide food and clothes for us, without which life could not be sustained on earth. God ordered the seasons—they are his will. In fact, the good things in life far outweigh the bad. There are more sunrises than cyclones.

— CHARLES L. ALLEN

If you would convince a man that he does wrong, do right. Men will believe what they see.

— HENRY DAVID THOREAU

The ego, as a collection of our past experiences, is continually offering miserable lines of thought. It's as if there were a stream with little fish swimming by, and when we hook one of them there is a judgement. The ego is constantly judging everybody and everything. It has its constant little chit chat about things that can happen in the future, things about the past, too, and these are the little fish that swim by. And what we learn to do—this is why it takes work— is to *not* reach out and grab a fish.

— HUGH PRATHER

I have made a ceaseless effort not to ridicule, not to bewail, not to scorn human actions, but to understand them.

— SPINOZA

Keep away from people who try to belittle your ambitions. Small people always do that, but the really great make you feel that you, too, can become great.

— MARK TWAIN

I ought to reflect again and again, and yet again, that the beings among whom I have to steer are just as inevitable in the scheme of evolution as I am myself; have just as much right to be themselves as I am entitled to; and they all deserve from me as much sympathy as I give to myself.

— ARNOLD BENNETT

It is healthier to see the good points of others than to analyze our own bad ones.

— FRANÇOISE SAGAN

Always keep in mind the part that mood can play in affecting one's judgment of a piece of work; be cautious of enthusiasm when the sun shines bright, and slow to dismissal when the clouds hang low.

— J. DONALD ADAMS

God himself, sir, does not propose to judge a man until his life is over. Why should you and I?

— SAMUEL JOHNSON

♦

If it is very painful for you to criticize your friends, you are safe in doing it. But if you take the slightest pleasure in it, that is the time to hold your tongue.

— ALICE MILLER

♦

Wanted: More Praise
I cannot help believing that the world will be a better and a happier place when people are praised more and blamed less; when we utter in their hearing the good we think and also gently intimate the criticisms we hope may be of service. For the world grows smaller every day. It will be but a family circle after a while.

— FRANCIS E. WILLARD

♦

How seldom we weigh our neighbor in the same balance with ourselves.

— THOMAS À KEMPIS

♦

The human race is divided into two classes — those that go ahead and do something and those who sit still and inquire, "Why wasn't it done the other way?"

— OLIVER WENDELL HOLMES, JR.

Prayer
Dear Lord of gracious mind and heart, forgive me for the unbearable ways of my arrogance and snobbishness. How unkind of me to think poorly without cause of those about me! Help me realize that a song can be lovely even though I neither wrote nor sang it. Make clear to me that all worthy thoughts did not originate in my mind; that other folk have good manners; and that when I pass away the world will not be bereft of grace and good breeding.

— ALLEN A. STOCKDALE

♦

He has the right to criticize who has the heart to help.

— ABRAHAM LINCOLN

♦

A man takes contradiction and advice much more easily than people think, only he will not bear it when violently given, even if it is well-founded. Hearts are like flowers; they remain open to the softly falling dew, but shut up in the violent downpour of rain.

— GEORGE MATTHEW ADAMS

♦

Why then do you criticize your brother's actions, why do you try to make him look small?

— ROMANS 14:10

Determination

O Lord,
you give us everything,
at the price of an effort.

Leonardo da Vinci

Get a good idea and stay with it.
Dog it, and work at it until it's done,
and done right.

— WALT DISNEY

♦

Prayer for Strength
This is my prayer to thee, my Lord —
Strike, strike at the root of penury in
my heart.
Give me the strength lightly to bear
my joys and sorrows.
Give me the strength to make my love
fruitful in service.
Give me the strength never to disown
the poor or bend my knees before
insolent might.
Give me the strength to raise my mind
high above daily trifles.
And give me the strength to surrender
my strength to thy will with love.

— RABINDRANATH TAGORE

♦

There is in this world no such force as
the force of a man determined to rise.
The human soul cannot be permanently
chained.

— W. E. B. DU BOIS

♦

The difficult we do immediately; the
impossible takes a little longer.

— AIR FORCE MOTTO

Always have the situation under control,
even if losing. Never betray an inward
sense of defeat.

— ARTHUR ASHE

♦

I do the very best I know how — the very
best I can; and I mean to keep doing so
until the end. If the end brings me out
right, what is said against me won't
amount to anything. If the end brings
me out wrong, ten angels swearing I
was right would make no difference.

— ABRAHAM LINCOLN

♦

I won't have any money to leave behind.
I won't have the fine and luxurious
things of life to leave behind. But I just
want to leave a committed life behind.

— MARTIN LUTHER KING, JR.

♦

I might have been born in a hovel, but
I determined to travel with the wind
and the stars.

— JACQUELINE COCHRAN

♦

To reach the port of heaven we must
sail, sometimes with the wind and
sometimes against it — but we must
sail, not drift or lie at anchor.

— OLIVER WENDELL HOLMES

By perseverance the snail reached
the ark.

— C. H. SPURGEON

♦

Weak men are the slaves of what happens. Strong men are masters of what
happens. Weak men are victims of their
environment. Strong men are victors in
any environment. Strong men may not
change the circumstances, but they will
use them, compel them to serve, and
bend them to their purposes. They may
not be able to change the direction of
the wind, but somehow they will coerce
the wind to fill their sails while they
drive the tiller over to keep their course.

— GEORGE CRAIG STEWART

♦

The cynic says "One man can't do
anything." I say "Only one man can
do anything."

— JOHN GARDNER

♦

Constant dripping hollows out a stone.

— LUCRETIUS

♦

The rung of a ladder was never meant
to rest upon, but only to hold a man's
foot long enough to enable him to put
the other somewhat higher.

— THOMAS HENRY HUXLEY

Risk! Risk anything! Care no more for
the opinion of others, for those voices.
Do the hardest thing on earth for you.
Act for yourself! Face the truth.

— KATHERINE MANSFIELD

♦

Prayer
Great God, I ask thee for no meaner pelf
Than that I may not disappoint myself.
That in my action I may soar as high
As I can now discern with this clear eye.

— HENRY DAVID THOREAU

♦

However confused the scene of our
   life appears,
however torn we may be who now
   do face that scene,
it can be faced, and we can go on
   to be whole.

— MURIEL RUKEYSER

♦

There is no such thing as a great talent
without great will-power.

— HONORÉ DE BALZAC

♦

With all the infinite possibilities of
spiritual life before you, do not settle
down on a little patch of dusty ground
at the mountain's foot in restful content.
Be not content until you reach the
mountain's summit.

— J. R. MILLER

This shall be my parting word: Know what you want to do—then do it. Make straight for your goal and go undefeated in spirit to the end.

— ERNESTINE SCHUMANN-HEINK

♦

Great things are done when men and mountains meet.

— WILLIAM BLAKE

♦

There are but two roads that lead to an important goal and to the doing of great things: strength and perseverance. Strength is the lot of but a few privileged men; but austere perseverance, harsh and continuous, may be employed by the smallest of us and rarely fails of its purpose, for *its silent power grows irresistibly greater with time.*

— JOHANN WOLFGANG
VON GOETHE

♦

If enough people think of a thing and work hard enough at it, I guess it's pretty nearly bound to happen, wind and weather permitting.

— LAURA INGALLS WILDER

♦

Kites rise against, not with, the wind. No man ever worked his passage anywhere in a dead calm.

— JOHN NEAL

What counts now is not just what we are against, but what we are for. Who leads us is less important than what leads us—what convictions, what courage, what faith—win or lose.

— ADLAI STEVENSON

♦

As the sculptor devotes himself to wood and stone, I would devote myself to my soul.

— TOYOHIKO KAGAWA

♦

We must accept responsibility for a problem before we can solve it. We cannot solve a problem by saying "It's not my problem," and hoping that someone else will solve it for us. We can solve a problem only when we say "This is *my* problem and it's up to me to solve it."

— M. SCOTT PECK

♦

The drop of rain maketh a hole in the stone, not by violence, but by oft falling.

— HUGH LATIMER

♦

I know of no more encouraging fact than the unquestionable ability of man to elevate his life by a conscious endeavor.

— HENRY DAVID THOREAU

Education

If you have knowledge,
let others light their candles at it.

Thomas Fuller

I am not a teacher, but an awakener.

— ROBERT FROST

◆

Education and Instruction

Education consists in preparing the moral character of a child, in teaching him the few fundamental and invariable principles accepted in all the countries of the world. It consists in giving him, from tenderest childhood, the notion of human dignity. On the other hand, instruction consists in making him absorb the accumulated knowledge of man in every realm. Education directs his actions, inspires his behavior in all his contacts with mankind, and helps him to master himself. Instruction gives him the elements of his intellectual activity and informs him of the actual state of his civilization. Education gives him the unalterable foundations of his life; instruction enables him to adapt himself to the variations of his environment and to link these variations to past and future events.

— PIERRE LECOMTE DU NOÜY

◆

I call a complete and generous education that which fits a man to perform justly, skillfully, and magnanimously all the offices, both private and public, of peace and war.

— JOHN MILTON

Thoughts reduced to paper are generally nothing more than the footprints of a man walking in the sand. It is true that we see the path that he has taken; but to know what he saw on the way, we must use our own eyes.

— ARTHUR SCHOPENHAUER

◆

History is the witness of the times, the torch of truth, the life of memory, the teacher of life, the messenger of antiquity.

— CARTER G. WOODSON

◆

Release

Every piece of marble has a statue in it waiting to be released by a man of sufficient skill to chip away the unnecessary parts. Just as the sculptor is to the marble, so is education to the soul. It releases it. For only educated men are free men. You cannot create a statue by smashing the marble with a hammer, and you cannot by force of arms release the spirit or the soul of man.

— CONFUCIUS

◆

Education does not mean teaching people to know what they do not know; it means teaching them to behave as they do not behave.

— JOHN RUSKIN

The great difficulty in education is to get experience out of ideas.

— GEORGE SANTAYANA

♦

Absolute Trust

All a child's life depends on the ideal it has of its parents. Destroy that and everything goes — morals, behavior, everything. Absolute trust in someone else is the essence of education.

— E. M. FORSTER

♦

The secret of education lies in respecting the pupil.

— RALPH WALDO EMERSON

♦

The man who does not read good books has no advantage over the man who can't read them.

— MARK TWAIN

♦

The entire object of true education is to make people not merely to do the right things, but enjoy them; not merely industrious, but to love industry; not merely learned, but to love knowledge; not merely pure, but to love purity; not merely just, but to hunger and thirst after justice.

— JOHN RUSKIN

There is nothing more remarkable in the life of Socrates than that he found time in his old age to learn to dance and play on instruments, and thought it was time well spent.

— MONTAIGNE

♦

In a democracy, education should be of value to men and women both as private individuals and as free, self-reliant, and responsible members of the community to which they belong. It should help them, as individuals, to grow in self-mastery and personal depth, to develop wider and deeper appreciations, to acquire an enthusiasm for hard work, to love good talk and good books, to delight in the adventures of intellectual curiosity, to become fair-minded, open-minded, and generous in all their human responses.

— ASSOCIATION OF AMERICAN COLLEGES

♦

It is a rare privilege to watch the birth, growth, and first feeble struggles of a living mind.

— ANNIE SULLIVAN

♦

Life is like playing a violin solo in public and learning the instrument as one goes on.

— SAMUEL BUTLER

A *Learner*

Each day I learn more than I teach;
I learn that half knowledge of another's
    life leads to false judgment;
I learn that there is a surprising kinship
    in human nature;
I learn that it's a wise father who knows
    his own son;
I learn that what we expect we get;
I learn that there's more good than evil
    in this world;
That age is a question of spirit;
That youth is the best of life no matter
    how numerous its years;
I learn how much there is to learn.

— VIRGINIA CHURCH

♦

As far as the education of children is
concerned I think they should be taught
not the little virtues but the great ones.
Not thrift but generosity and an indifference to money; not caution but
courage and a contempt for danger; not
shrewdness but frankness and a love of
truth; not tact but love for one's neighbor and self-denial; not a desire for
success but a desire to be and to know.

— NATALIA GINZBURG

♦

Man is obviously made to think. It is his
whole dignity and his whole merit; and
his whole duty is to think as he ought.

— BLAISE PASCAL

Throughout education there is a great
amount of pumping into you, so to
speak. Now, the best part of education
is giving something out from you. Let
something of thought and imagination
issue from you. Think independently,
so far as you can; in youth not so much
as in adult age, but begin in youth the
process of independent thought.

— CHARLES ELIOT

♦

Education is the ability to listen to
almost anything without losing your
temper or your self-esteem.

— ROBERT FROST

♦

Frontiers

We often think of ourselves as living in
a world which no longer has any unex-
plored frontiers. We speak of pioneering
as a thing of the past. But in doing so
we forget that the greatest adventure of
all still challenges us — what Mr. Justice
Holmes called "the adventure of the
human mind." Men may be hemmed
in geographically, but every generation
stands on the frontiers of the mind. In
the world of ideas, there is always pioneering to be done, and it can be done
by anyone who will use the equipment
with which he is endowed. The great
ideas belong to everyone.

— MORTIMER J. ADLER

Faith

Whoso draws nigh to God
one step through doubtings dim,
God will advance a mile
in blazing light to him.

Never Forsaken

God is the hardest taskmaster I have
known on this earth, and he tries you
through and through. And when you
find that your faith is failing or your
body is failing you, and you are sinking,
he comes to your assistance somehow or
other and proves to you that you must
not lose your faith and that he is always
at your beck and call, but on his terms,
not on your terms. So I have found.
I cannot really recall a single instance
when, at the eleventh hour, he has
forsaken me.

— MAHATMA GANDHI

◆

Faith is an act of rational choice which
determines us to act as if certain things
were true and in the confident expectation that they will prove to be true.

—WILLIAM R. INGE

◆

The most important element in human
life is faith; if God were to take away
all His blessings — health, physical
fitness, wealth, intelligence — and leave
me with but one gift I would ask him
for faith. For with faith in Him and His
goodness, mercy and love for me, and
belief in everlasting life, I believe I could
suffer the loss of all my other gifts and
still be happy.

— ROSE KENNEDY

Who has seen the wind?
Neither you nor I;
But when the trees bow down
    their heads,
The wind is passing by.

— CHRISTINA ROSSETTI

◆

Faith⹀Ladder

A conception of the world arises in you
    somehow, no matter how. Is it true
    or not? you ask.
It *might* be true somewhere, you say, for
    it is not self-contradictory.
It *may* be true, you continue, even here
    and now.
It is *fit* to be true, it would be *well if it
    were true,* it *ought* to be true, you
    presently feel.
It *must* be true, something persuasive
    in you whispers next; and then — as
    a final result —
It shall be *held for true,* you decide; it
    shall be as if true, for *you.*
And your acting thus may in certain
    special cases be a means of making
    it securely true in the end.

— WILLIAM JAMES

◆

The universe was not made in jest but
in solemn incomprehensible earnest. By
a power that is unfathomably secret, and
holy, and fleet.

— ANNIE DILLARD

A word has power in and of itself. It comes from nothing into sound and meaning; it gives origin to all things. By means of the word can a man deal with the world on equal terms. And the word is sacred.

— N. SCOTT MOMADAY

Faith . . . is nothing at all tangible. It is simply believing God; and, like sight, it is nothing apart from its object. You might as well shut your eyes and look inside, and see whether you have sight, as to look inside to discover whether you have faith.

— HANNAH WHITALL SMITH

Faith is not belief without proof, but trust without reservations.

— ELTON TRUEBLOOD

Yes, I have doubted. I have wandered off the path. I have been lost. But I have always returned. It is beyond the logic I seek. It is intuitive — an intrinsic, built-in sense of direction. I seem to always find my way home. My faith has wavered but has saved me.

— HELEN HAYES

Christ must be rediscovered perpetually.

— EDITH HAMILTON

What Christ Asks
The best definition of faith that I know is that it is reason grown courageous. Moreover, that is all that Christ ever asked us for, and the reason that he asked us for that was because he wants to use us. He needs our help. It is almost impossible to believe it, but God Almighty wants our help, so Christ tells us. Theoretically or mathematically this is unintelligible, that God should want human help. But this is the bottom of all Christ's teaching. The faith he asks for is not to understand him but to follow him. By that and that alone can man convert the tragedy of human life, full of disappointments, disillusionments, and with so-called death ever looming ahead, into the most glorious field of honor, worthy of the dignity of a son of God. What Christ asks is that we shall try it out. He actually dares us to follow him. In that way, he says, you shall win that prize in life, for which any man can with perfect reason afford to give everything else.

— WILFRED T. GRENFELL

He who is swift to believe is swift to forget.

— ABRAHAM JOSHUA HESCHEL

The steps of faith fall on the seeming void and find the rock beneath.

— WALT WHITMAN

♦

Lost and Found

I missed him when the sun began
    to bend;
I found him not when I had lost
    his rim;
With many tears I went in search
    of him,
Climbing high mountains which
    did still ascend,
And gave me echoes when I called
    my friend;
Through cities vast and charnel-
    houses grim,
And high cathedrals where the light
    was dim,
Through books and arts and works
    without an end,
But found him not—the friend whom
    I had lost.
And yet I found him—as I found
    the lark,
A sound in fields I heard but could
    not mark;
I found him in my heart, a life in frost,
A light I knew not till my soul was dark.

— GEORGE MACDONALD

♦

To lose faith in our fellow men is the unforgivable sin.

— JOHN DEWEY

It is only in the lonely emergencies of life that our creed is tested: the routine maxims fail, and we fall back on our gods.

— WILLIAM JAMES

♦

What keeps our faith cheerful is the extreme persistence of gentleness and humor. Gentleness is everywhere in daily life, a sign that faith rules through ordinary things: through cooking and small talk, through storeytelling, making love, fishing, tending animals and sweet corn and flowers, through sports, music, and books, raising kids—all the places where the gravy soaks in and grace shines through. Even in a time of elephantine vanity and greed, one never has to look far to see the campfires of gentle people. Lacking any other purpose in life, it would be good enough to live for their sake.

— GARRISON KEILLOR

♦

How could we search for God, since He is above, in a dimension not open to us? . . . We must only wait and call out.

— SIMONE WEIL

♦

Belief . . . is the engine that makes perception operate.

— FLANNERY O'CONNOR

Family

Lord, this humble house we'd keep
Sweet with play and calm with sleep.
Help us so that we may give
Beauty to the lives we live.
Let Thy love and let Thy grace
Shine upon our dwelling place.

Edgar A. Guest

The family—that dear octopus from whose tentacles we never quite escape, nor, in our inmost hearts, ever quite wish to.

—DODIE SMITH

♦

What Is Home?
A roof to keep out the rain. Four walls to keep out the wind. Floors to keep out the cold. Yes, but home is more than that. It is the laugh of a baby, the song of a mother, the strength of a father. Warmth of loving hearts, light from happy eyes, kindness, loyalty, comradeship. Home is first school and first church for young ones, where they learn what is right, what is good, and what is kind. Where they go for comfort when they are hurt or sick. Where joy is shared and sorrow eased. Where fathers and mothers are respected and loved. Where children are wanted. Where the simplest food is good enough for kings because it is earned. Where money is not so important as loving-kindness. Where even the teakettle sings from happiness. That is home. God bless it.

—ERNESTINE SCHUMAN-HEINK

♦

Your success as family, our success as a society, depends not on what happens in the White House, but on what happens inside your house.

—BARBARA BUSH

Marriage
Perhaps the greatest blessing in marriage is that it lasts so long. The years, like the varying interests of each year, combine to buttress and enrich each other. Out of many shared years, one life. In a series of temporary relationships, one misses the ripening, gathering, harvesting joys, the deep, hard-won truths of marriage.

—RICHARD C. CABOT

♦

Perhaps the greatest social service that can be rendered by anybody to this country and to mankind is to bring up a family.

—GEORGE BERNARD SHAW

♦

All of childhood's unanswered questions must finally be passed back to [one's hometown] and answered there. Heroes and bogey men, values and dislikes, are first encountered and labeled in that early environment. In later years they change faces, places, and maybe races, tactics, intensities and goals, but beneath the penetrable masks they wear forever the stocking-capped faces of childhood.

—MAYA ANGELOU

♦

The mother's heart is the child's schoolroom.

—HENRY WARD BEECHER

A *Father's Prayer*

Build me a son, O Lord, who will be
strong enough to know when he is
weak, and brave enough to face himself
when he is afraid; one who will be proud
and unbending in honest defeat, and
humble and gentle in victory.

Build me a son whose wishbone will
not be where his backbone should be;
a son who will know thee and that to
know himself is the foundation stone
of knowledge.

Lead him, I pray, not in the path of
ease and comfort, but under the stress
and spur of difficulties and challenge.
Here let him learn to stand up in the
storm; here let him learn compassion
for those who fail.

Build me a son whose heart will be
clear, whose goal will be high; a son who
will master himself before he seeks to
master other men; one who will learn to
laugh, yet never forget how to weep; one
who will reach into the future, yet never
forget the past.

And after all these things are his, add,
I pray, enough of a sense of humor, so
that he may always be serious, yet never
take himself too seriously. Give him humility, so that he may always remember
the simplicity of true greatness, the open
mind of true wisdom, the meekness of
true strength.

Then I, his father, will dare to whisper, "I have not lived in vain."

— DOUGLAS MACARTHUR

Home is not where you live but where
they understand you.

— CHRISTIAN MORGENSTERN

•

A good marriage is that in which
each appoints the other guardian
of his solitude.

— RAINER MARIA RILKE

•

Let parents bequeath to their children
not riches, but the spirit of reverence.

— PLATO

•

Confident *Living*

Home is the one place in all this world
where hearts are sure of each other. It
is the place of confidence. It is the place
where we tear off that mask of guarded
and suspicious coldness which the world
forces us to wear in self-defense, and
where we pour out the unreserved com-
munications of full and confiding hearts.
It is the spot where expressions of tenderness gush out without any sensation
of awkwardness and without any dread
of ridicule.

— FREDERICK W. ROBERTSON

•

What families have in common the
world around is that they are the place
where people learn who they are and
how to be that way.

— JEAN ILLSLEY CLARKE

Science has established two facts meaningful for human welfare: first, the foundation of the structure of human personality is laid down in early childhood; and second, the chief engineer in charge of this construction is the family.

— MEYER FRANCIS NIMKOFF

◆

Family Worship
There is one practice which any family can maintain and that is the practice of a time of worship at each family meal. Nearly all families are together for at least one meal a day and, in any case, should sacrifice much else to make this possible. *The table is really the family altar!* Here those of all ages come together and help to sustain both their physical and their spiritual existence. If a sacrament is "an actual conveyance of spiritual meaning and power by a material process," then a family meal can be a sacrament. It entwines the material and the spiritual in a remarkable way. The food, in and of itself, is purely physical, but it represents human service in its use. Here, at one common table, is the father who has earned, the mother who has prepared or planned, and the children who share, according to need, whatever their antecedent participation may have been.

When we realize how deeply a meal together can be a spiritual and regenerating experience, we can understand something of why our Lord, when he broke bread with his little company toward the end of their earthly fellowship, told them, as often as they did it, to remember him. We, too, seek to be members of his sacred fellowship, and irrespective of what we do about the Eucharist, there is no reason why each family meal should not take on something of the character of a time of memory and hope.

— ELTON TRUEBLOOD

◆

I have come back again to where I belong; not an enchanted place, but the walls are strong.

— DOROTHY H. RATH

◆

To nourish children and raise them against odds is in any time, any place, more valuable than to fix bolts in cars or design nuclear weapons.

— MARILYN FRENCH

◆

The world tips away when we look in our children's faces.

— LOUISE ERDRICH

◆

Both within the family and without, our sisters hold up our mirrors: our images of who we are and of who we can dare to become.

— ELIZABETH FISHELL

A man builds a fine house; and now he has a master, and a task for life is to furnish, watch, show it, and keep it in repair the rest of his life.

— RALPH WALDO EMERSON

◆

Devotion
There is an enduring tenderness in the love of a mother to a son that transcends all other affections of the heart. It is neither to be chilled by selfishness, nor daunted by danger, nor weakened by worthlessness, nor stifled by ingratitude. She will sacrifice every comfort to his convenience; she will surrender every pleasure to his enjoyment; she will glory in his fame and exult in his prosperity; and if adversity overtake him, he will be the dearer to her by misfortune; and if disgrace settle upon his name, she will still love and cherish him; and if all the world beside cast him off, she will be all the world to him.

— WASHINGTON IRVING

◆

No music is so pleasant to my ears as that word — father.

— LYDIA MARIA CHILD

◆

Parents have become so convinced that educators know what is best for their children that they forget that they themselves are really the experts.

— MARIAN WRIGHT EDELMAN

Family life is full of major and minor crises — the ups and downs of health, success and failure in career, marriage, and divorce — and all kinds of characters. It is tied to places and events and histories. With all of these felt details, life etches itself into memory and personality. It's difficult to imagine anything more nourishing to the soul.

— THOMAS MOORE

◆

A house may draw visitors, but it is the possessor alone that can detain them.

— CHARLES CALEB COLTON

◆

Tribute to a Mother
Faith that withstood the shocks of toil
    and time;
  Hope that defied despair;
  Patience that conquered care;
And loyalty, whose courage was sublime;
The great deep heart that was a home
    for all —
  Just, eloquent, and strong
  In protest against wrong;
Wide charity, that knew no sin, no fall;
The Spartan spirit that made life so
    grand,
  Mating poor daily needs
  With high, heroic deeds,
That wrested happiness from Fate's hard
    hand.

— LOUISA MAY ALCOTT

Every generation revolts against its fathers and makes friends with its grandfathers.

— LEWIS MUMFORD

Example

From the services in which I joined as a child I have taken with me into life a feeling for what is solemn, and a need for quiet self-recollection, without which I cannot realize the meaning of my life. I cannot, therefore, support the opinion of those who would not let children take part in grown-up people's services till they to some extent understand them. The important thing is not that they shall understand but that they shall feel something of what is serious and solemn. The fact that a child sees his elders full of devotion, and has to feel something of devotion himself, that is what gives the service its meaning for him.

— ALBERT SCHWEITZER

Marriage is not just spiritual communion and passionate embraces; marriage is also three-meals-a-day and remembering to carry the garbage out.

— JOYCE BROTHERS

Behold! how good and pleasant it is for brethren to dwell together in unity!

— PSALM 133:1

It seems to me that since I've had children, I've grown richer and deeper. They may have slowed down my writing for a while, but when I did write, I had more of a self to speak from.

— ANNE TYLER

Sisters is probably the most competitive relationship within the family, but once the sisters are grown up, it becomes the strongest relationship.

— MARGARET MEAD

Happy marriages begin when we marry the ones we love, and they blossom when we love the ones we marry.

— TOM MULLEN

Only One Mother

Most of all the other beautiful things in life come by twos and threes, by dozens and hundreds. Plenty of roses, stars, sunsets, rainbows, brothers and sisters, aunts and cousins, but only one mother in the whole world.

— KATE DOUGLAS WIGGIN

A mother is not a person to lean on but a person to make leaning unnecessary.

— DOROTHY CANFIELD FISHER

Friendship

I didn't find my friends;
the good God gave them to me.

Ralph Waldo Emerson

A friend is a present you give yourself.

— ROBERT LOUIS STEVENSON

♦

Discussing the character and foibles of common friends is a great sweetener and cement of friendship.

— WILLIAM HAZLITT

♦

Friendship is more delicate than love. Quarrels and fretful complaints are attractive in the last, offensive in the first. And the very things which heap fuel on the fire of ardent passion, choke and extinguish sober and true regard. On the other hand, time, which is sure to *destroy* that love of which half certainly depends on *desire,* is as sure to increase friendship founded on talents, warm with esteem, and ambitious of success for the object of it.

— HESTER LYNCH PIOZZI

♦

The truth is friendship is to me every bit as sacred and eternal as marriage.

— KATHERINE MANSFIELD

♦

A true friend unbosoms freely, advises justly, assists readily, adventures boldly, takes all patiently, defends courageously, and continues a friend unchangeably.

— WILLIAM PENN

We soon cease to feel the grief at the deaths of our friends, yet we continue to the end of our lives to miss them. They are still with us in their absence.

— GERALD BRENAN

♦

There was a definite process by which one made people into friends, and it involved talking to them and listening to them for hours at a time.

— REBECCA WEST

♦

We cannot tell the precise moment when friendship is formed. As in filling a vessel drop by drop, there is at last a drop which makes it run over; so in a series of kindnesses there is at last one which makes the heart run over.

— SAMUEL JOHNSON

♦

Old friends are the best. King James used to call for his old shoes; they were easiest for his feet.

— JOHN SELDEN

♦

We take care of our health, we lay up money, we make our room tight, and our clothing sufficient; but who provides wisely that he shall not be wanting in the best property of all — friends?

— RALPH WALDO EMERSON

The Arrow and the Song

I shot an arrow into the air,
It fell to earth, I knew not where;
For, so swiftly it flew, the sight
Could not follow it in its flight.

I breathed a song into the air,
It fell to earth, I knew not where;
For who has sight so keen and strong,
That it can follow the flight of song?

Long, long afterward, in an oak
I found the arrow, still unbroke;
And the song, from beginning to end,
I found again in the heart of a friend.

— HENRY WADSWORTH
LONGFELLOW

♦

One's friends are that part of the human race with which one can be human.

— GEORGE SANTAYANA

♦

Friendship is a sheltering tree.

— SAMUEL TAYLOR COLERIDGE

♦

It is the steady and merciless increase of occupations, the augmented speed at which we are always trying to live, the crowding of each day with more work than it can profitably hold, which has cost us, among other things, the undisturbed enjoyment of friends. Friendship takes time, and we have no time to give it.

— AGNES REPPLIER
(1894)

Oh, the comfort, the inexpressible comfort of feeling safe with a person; having neither to weigh thoughts nor measure words, but to pour them all out, just as they are, chaff and grain together, knowing that a faithful hand will take and sift them, keep what is worth keeping, and then, with the breath of kindness, blow the rest away.

— GEORGE ELIOT

♦

People are lonely because they build walls instead of bridges.

— JOSEPH FORT NEWTON

♦

"Stay" is a charming word in a friend's vocabulary.

— AMOS BRONSON ALCOTT

♦

Your friends will know you better in the first minute you meet than your acquaintances will know you in a thousand years.

— RICHARD BACH

♦

Except in cases of necessity, which are rare, leave your friend to learn unpleasant things from his enemies; they are ready enough to tell him.

— OLIVER WENDELL HOLMES

Mending Wall

Something there is that doesn't love a wall,
That sends the frozen-ground-swell under it,
And spills the upper boulders in the sun;
And makes gaps even two can pass abreast.
The work of hunters is another thing:
I have come after them and made repair
Where they have left not one stone on a stone,
But they would have the rabbit out of hiding,
To please the yelping dogs. The gaps I mean,
No one has seen them made or heard them made,
But at spring mending-time we find them there.
I let my neighbor know beyond the hill;
And on a day we meet to walk the line
And set the wall between us once again.
We keep the wall between us as we go.
To each the boulders that have fallen to each.
And some are loaves and some so nearly balls
We have to use a spell to make them balance:
"Stay where you are until our backs are turned!"
We wear our fingers rough with handling them.
Oh, just another kind of outdoor game,
One on a side. It comes to little more:
There where it is we do not need the wall:
He is all pine and I am apple-orchard.

My apple trees will never get across
And eat the cones under his pines, I tell him.
He only says, "Good fences make good neighbors."
Spring is the mischief in me, and I wonder
If I could put a notion in his head:
"*Why* do they make good neighbors? Isn't it
Where there are cows? But here there are no cows.
Before I built a wall I'd ask to know
What I was walling in or walling out,
And to whom I was like to give offense.
Something there is that doesn't love a wall,
That wants it down!" I could say "Elves" to him,
But it's not elves exactly, and I'd rather
He said it for himself. I see him there
Bringing a stone grasped firmly by the top
In each hand, like an old-stone savage armed.
He moves in darkness, as it seems to me,
Not of woods only and the shade of trees.
He will not go behind his father's saying,
And he likes having thought of it so well
He says again, "Good fences make good neighbors."

— ROBERT FROST

So long as we love, we serve; so long as we are loved by others, I should say that we are almost indispensable; and no man is useless while he has a friend.

—ROBERT LOUIS STEVENSON

Be slow in choosing a friend, slower in changing.

—BENJAMIN FRANKLIN

[A] workable and effective way to meet and overcome difficulties is to take on someone else's problems. It is a strange fact but you can often handle two difficulties—your own and somebody else's—better than you can handle your own alone. That truth is based on a subtle law of self-giving or outgoingness whereby you develop a self-strengthening in the process.

—NORMAN VINCENT PEALE

Am I united with my friend in heart? What matters if our place be wide apart?

—ANWAR-I-SUHEILI

Don't flatter yourself that friendship authorizes you to say disagreeable things to your intimates. The nearer you come into relation with a person, the more necessary do tact and courtesy become.

—OLIVER WENDELL HOLMES

Silences make the real conversations between friends. Not the saying but the never needing to say is what counts.

—MARGARET LEE RUNBECK

If a man does not make new acquaintances as he advances through life, he will soon find himself left alone. A man should keep his friendship in constant repair.

—SAMUEL JOHNSON

Think where man's glory most
   begins and ends
And say that my glory was I had
   such friends.

—WILLIAM BUTLER YEATS

Few delights can equal the mere presence of one whom we trust utterly.

—GEORGE MACDONALD

The most I can do for my friend is simply to be his friend. I have no wealth to bestow on him. If he knows that I am happy in loving him, he will want no other reward. Is not friendship divine in this?

—HENRY DAVID THOREAU

Gifts

Blessed are those who can
give without remembering and
take without forgetting.

Elizabeth Bibesco

We are rich only through what we give and poor only through what we refuse.

— ANNE-SOPHIE SWETCHINE

♦

Give what you have. To some one, it may be better than you dare to think.

— HENRY WADSWORTH
LONGFELLOW

♦

The Golden Ladder of Giving

1. To give reluctantly, the gift of the hand, but not of the heart.
2. To give cheerfully, but not in proportion to need.
3. To give cheerfully and proportionately, but not until solicited.
4. To give cheerfully, proportionately, and unsolicited, but to put the gift into the poor man's hand, thus creating shame.
5. To give in such a way that the distressed may know their benefactor, without being known to him.
6. To know the objects of our bounty, but remain unknown to them.
7. To give so that the benefactor may not know those whom he has relieved, and they shall not know him.
8. To prevent poverty by teaching a trade, setting a man up in business, or in some other way preventing the need of charity.

— MAIMONIDES

But what parent can tell when some . . . fragmentary gift of knowledge or wisdom will enrich her children's lives? Or how a small seed of information passed from one generation to another may generate a new science, a new industry — a seed which neither the giver nor the receiver can truly evaluate at the time.

— HELENA RUBINSTEIN

♦

A man has made at least a start on discovering the meaning of human life when he plants shade trees under which he knows full well he will never sit.

— ELTON TRUEBLOOD

♦

A Song of Service
If all my pain and all my tears,
And all that I have learned
    throughout the years
Could make one perfect song
To lift some fallen head
To light some darkened mind,
I should feel that not in vain
I served mankind.

— MARGUERITE FEW

♦

I have held many things in my hands, and I have lost them all; but whatever I have placed in God's hands, that I still possess.

— MARTIN LUTHER

Lord, make me a channel of thy peace
That where there is hatred I may
    bring love,
That where there is wrong I may
    bring the spirit of forgiveness,
That where there is discord I may
    bring harmony,
That where there is error I may
    bring truth,
That where there is doubt I may
    bring faith,
That where there is despair I may
    bring hope,
That where there are shadows I may
    bring thy light,
That where there is sadness I may
    bring joy.

Lord, grant that I may seek rather
To comfort—than to be comforted;
To understand—than to be understood;
To love—than to be loved;
For it is by giving that one receives;
It is by self-forgetting that one finds;
It is by forgiving that one is forgiven;
It is by dying that one awakens to
    eternal life.

    —ST. FRANCIS OF ASSISI

◆

A cheerful giver does not count the
cost of what he gives. His heart is set on
pleasing and cheering him to whom the
gift is given.

    —JULIAN OF NORWICH

Not what we give, but what we share,—
For the gift without the giver is bare;
Who gives himself with his alms feeds
    three,—
Himself, his hungering neighbor,
    and Me.

    —JAMES RUSSELL LOWELL

◆

Of all the dear sights in the world, nothing is so beautiful as a child when it is
giving something. Any small thing it
gives. A child gives the world to you.
It opens the world to you as if it were
a book you'd never been able to read.
But when a gift must be found, it is always some absurd little thing, pasted
on crooked . . . an angel looking like a
clown. A child has so little that it can
give, because it never knows it has
given you everything.

    —MARGARET LEE RUNBECK

◆

God's gifts put man's best dreams to
shame.

    —ELIZABETH BARRETT BROWNING

◆

As Coleridge said, "We receive but what
we give." The happy life is a life of con-
tinual generosity in which we go out to
meet and acclaim the world.

    —GERALD BRENAN

Gifts

Last Will and Testament

I, Charles Lounsbury, being of sound mind and disposing memory, do hereby make and publish this, my last will and testament, in order, as justly as I may, to distribute my interests in the world among succeeding men.

That part of my interests which is known in the law and recognized in the sheep-bound volumes as my property, being inconsiderable and of no account, I make no disposal of it in my will.

My right to live, being but a life estate, is not at my disposal, but, these excepted, all else in the world I now proceed to devise and bequeath.

Item: I give to good fathers and mothers, but in trust for their children all and every, the flowers of the fields and the blossoms of the woods, with the right to play among them freely, according to the custom of children, warning them at the same time against the thistles. And I devise to children the banks of the brooks, and the golden sands beneath the waters thereof, and the odors of the willows that dip therein, and the white clouds that float high over the giant trees. And I leave the children the long, long days to be merry in, in a thousand ways, and the night, and the moon, and the train of the Milky Way to wonder at, but subject, nevertheless, to the rights hereinafter given to lovers.

Item: I devise to boys jointly all the useful idle fields and commons where ball may be played; all pleasant waters where one may swim; all snow-clad hills where one may coast; and all streams and ponds where one may fish, or where, when grim winter comes, one may skate; to have and to hold the same for the period of their boyhood. And all meadows with the clover blossoms and butterflies thereof, the woods and their appurtenances, the squirrels, and birds, and echoes, and strange noises, and all distant places which may be visited, together with the adventures there found. And I give to said boys each his own place at the fireside at night, with all pictures that may be seen in the burning wood, to enjoy without let or hindrance, and without incumbrance of cares.

Item: To lovers I devise their imaginary world, with whatever they may need — the stars of the sky, the red roses by the wall, the bloom of the hawthorn, the sweet strains of music, and aught else by which they may desire to figure to each other the lastingness and beauty of their love.

Item: To young men jointly, I devise and bequeath all boisterous, inspiring sports of rivalry, and I give to them the disdain of weakness and undaunted confidence in their own strength. I give them the power to make lasting friendships, and of possessing companions, and to them exclusively I give all merry songs and brave choruses to sing with lusty voices.

Item: And to those who are no longer children or youths or lovers, I leave memory, and I bequeath to them the volumes of the poems of Burns and Shakespeare and of other poets, if there be others, to the end that they may live the old days again, freely and fully, without tithe or diminution. To our loved ones with snowy crowns I bequeath the happiness of old age, and the love and gratitude of their children.

Fulfilling work, rewarding relationships, personal power, and relief from symptoms are all gifts of the soul.

— THOMAS MOORE

◆

Giving

There are those who give little of the much they have — and they give it for recognition and their hidden desire makes their gifts unwholesome.

And there are those who have little and give it all.

These are the believers in life and the bounty of life, and their coffer is never empty.

There are those who give with joy, and that joy is their reward.

And there are those who give with pain, and that pain is their baptism.

And there are those who give and know not pain in giving, nor do they seek joy, nor give with mindfulness of virtue;

They give as in yonder valley the myrtle breathes its fragrance into space.

Through the hands of such as these God speaks, and from behind their eyes He smiles upon the earth.

— KAHLIL GIBRAN

◆

We start with gifts. Merit comes from what we make of them.

— JEAN TOOMER

He who has nothing can give nothing. The gift is God's — to God.

— DAG HAMMARSKJÖLD

◆

What can I give Him
Poor as I am?
If I were a shepherd,
I would give Him a lamb,
If I were a Wise Man,
I would do my part, —
But what I can I give Him,
Give my heart.

— CHRISTINA ROSSETTI

◆

A gift is as a precious stone in the eyes of him that hath it: whithersoever it turneth, it prospereth.

— PROVERBS 17:8

◆

Thou that hast given so much to me,
Give one thing more — a grateful heart;
Not thankful when it pleaseth me,
As if thy blessings had spare days;
But such a heart, whose pulse may be
Thy praise.

— GEORGE HERBERT

◆

We make a living by what we get, but we make a life by what we give.

— WINSTON CHURCHILL

Goodness

A saint is one who
makes goodness attractive.

Laurence Housman

Good actions are the invisible hinges on the doors of heaven.

—VICTOR HUGO

◆

Variations of the Golden Rule

One should seek for others the happiness one desires for one's self.

—BUDDHIST

What you would not wish done to yourself do not do unto others.

—CHINESE

Do not that to a neighbor which you shall take ill from him.

—GREEK

The true rule of life is to guard and do by the things of others as they do by their own.

—HINDU

Let none of you treat his brother in a way he himself would not like to be treated.

—MUSLIM

Do as you would be done by.

—PERSIAN

The law imprinted on the hearts of all men is to love the members of society as themselves.

—ROMAN

To me, one of the proofs that there is a moral governance in the universe is the fact that when men and governments work intelligently and far-sightedly for the good of others, they achieve their own prosperity too.

—BARABARA WARD

◆

Do all the good you can,
By all the means you can,
In all the ways you can,
In all the places you can,
At all the times you can,
To all the people you can,
As long as ever you can.

—JOHN WESLEY

◆

All that is good, all that is true, all that is beautiful, all that is beneficent, be it great or small, be it perfect or fragmentary, natural as well as supernatural, moral as well as material, comes from God.

—JOHN HENRY NEWMAN

◆

No man or woman can really be strong, gentle, pure, and good without the world being better for it.

—PHILLIPS BROOKS

She tended to be impatient with that sort of intellectual who, for all his brilliance, has never been able to arrive at the simple conclusion that to be reasonably happy you have to be reasonably good.

— CAROLYN KIZER

♦

Be not simply good; be good for something.

— HENRY DAVID THOREAU

♦

Don't be a cynic and bewail and
    bemoan. Omit the negative
    propositions.
Don't waste yourself in rejection,
    nor bark against the bad, but
    chant the beauty of the good.

— RALPH WALDO EMERSON

♦

The greatest pleasure I know is to do a good action by stealth and to have it found out by accident.

— CHARLES LAMB

♦

We ought to do good to others as simply and as naturally as a horse runs, or a bee makes honey, or a vine bears grapes season after season without thinking of the grapes it has borne.

— MARCUS AURELIUS

Prayer
Keep me, O Lord, from all pettiness.
    Let me be large in thought and
    word and deed.
Let me leave off self-seeking and have
    done with fault-finding.
Help me put away all pretense, that
    I may meet my neighbor face to
    face, without self-pity and without
    prejudice.
May I never be hasty in my judgments,
    but generous to all and in all things.
Make me grow calm, serene, and gentle.
Teach me to put into action my better
    impulses and make me straightfor-
    ward and unafraid.
Grant that I may realize that it is the
    trifling things of life that create
    differences, that in the higher
    things we are all one.
And, O Lord, God, let me not forget
    to be kind!

— MARY STUART

♦

All his earthly past will have been heaven to those who are saved. . . . The good man's past begins to change so that his forgiven sins and remembered sorrows take on the quality of heaven. . . . At the end of all things, the blessed will say, "We never lived anywhere but in heaven."

— C. S. LEWIS

What Is a Saint?

1. His life is imbued with a deep love of the Christian religion as a way of "feeling at home" in the universe.
2. He lives with a radiance because his spirit is rooted in God's Spirit. "A saint is a person who has quit worrying about himself" because his life is centered in God. With Jakob Böhme he says, "Though my head and my hand be at labor, yet doth my heart dwell in God."
3. He starts each day with these words: "May the image of Christ radiate through me this day in each life situation."
4. He asks that God use him as an instrument of his love to bear the burdens of his fellow men. Like Francis of Assisi, the saint loves "not humanity but men."
5. He believes that before God's kingdom can arrive in society, it must first begin in him.
6. He has humility, caused by his belief that life is too much trouble unless he can live for something that is big. And most of all, his life is lost in the bigness of God.
7. He feels that every person — regardless of color, race, creed, or nation — is a person in whom lie the possibilities of becoming a saint. With Robert Southwell he says, "Not where I breathe but where I love, I live."
8. He desires to use the results of prayer and devotion to better the world.
9. He believes that the two great secrets for becoming a saint lie in "the imitation of Christ" and "the practice of the presence of God."
10. His daily preparation for sainthood is in these words:

> By all means use some time to be alone.
> Salute thyself; see what thy soul doth wear.
> Dare to look into thy chest; for 'tis thy own.

—THOMAS S. KEPLER

♦

Conviction is worthless unless it is converted into conduct.

—THOMAS CARLYLE

♦

True Morality

Morality has been conceived up to the present in a very narrow spirit, as obedience to a law, as inner struggle between opposite laws. As for me, I declare that when I do good I obey no one, I fight no battle and win no victory. The cultivated man has only to follow the delicious incline of his inner impulses. Be beautiful and then do at each moment whatever your heart may inspire you to do. This is the whole of morality.

—ERNEST RENAN

Happiness

Happiness comes of the capacity
to feel deeply, to enjoy simply, to think freely,
to risk life, to be needed.

Storm Jameson

When one door of happiness closes another opens; but often we look so long at the closed door that we do not see the one which has been opened for us.

—HELEN KELLER

♦

Full Life

If you observe a really happy man you will find him building a boat, writing a symphony, educating his son, growing double dahlias in his garden, or looking for dinosaur eggs in the Gobi desert. He will not be searching for happiness as if it were a collar button that has rolled under the radiator. He will not be striving for it as a goal in itself. He will have become aware that he is happy in the course of living life twenty-four crowded hours of the day.

—W. BÉRAN WOLFE

♦

Everyday happiness means getting up in the morning and you can't wait to finish your breakfast. You can't wait to do your exercises. You can't wait to put on your clothes. To can't wait to get out—and you can't wait to come home, because the soup is hot.

—GEORGE BURNS

♦

We all live with the objective of being happy; our lives are all different and yet the same.

—ANNE FRANK

from *The Family Reunion*

I feel quite happy, as if happiness
Did not consist in getting what
  one wanted
Or in getting rid of what can't be
  got rid of
But in a different vision.

—T. S. ELIOT

♦

That is happiness; to be dissolved into something complete and great. When it comes to one, it comes as naturally as sleep.

—WILLA CATHER

♦

To find out what one is fitted to do and to secure an opportunity to do it is the key to happiness.

—JOHN DEWEY

♦

One road to happiness is to cultivate curiosity about everything. Not only about people but about subjects, not only about the arts but about history and foreign customs. Not only about countries and cities, but about plants and animals. Not only about lichened rocks and curious markings on the bark of trees, but about stars and atoms. Not only about our friends but about that strange labyrinth we inhabit which we call ourselves. Then, if we do that, we will never suffer a moment's boredom.

—GERALD BRENAN

There is an idea abroad among moral people that they should make their neighbors good. One person I have to make good: myself. But my duty to my neighbor is much more nearly expressed by saying that I must make him happy—if I may.

— ROBERT LOUIS STEVENSON

If one only wished to be happy, this could be easily accomplished; but we wish to be happier than other people, and this is always difficult, for we believe others to be happier than they are.

— MONTESQUIEU

That state of life is most happy where superfluities are not required and necessities are not wanting.

— PLUTARCH

Everybody really knows what to do to have his life filled with joy. What is it? Quit hating people; start loving them. Quit being mad at people; start liking them. Quit doing wrong; quit being filled with fear. Quit thinking about yourself and go out and do something for other people. Everybody knows what you have to do to be happy. But the wisdom of the test lies in the final words: "If ye know these things, *happy are ye if ye do them.*"

— NORMAN VINCENT PEALE

The year's at the spring
And day's at the morn;
Morning's at seven:
The hillside's dew-pearled;
The lark's on the wing;
The snail's on the thorn;
God's in his heaven—
All's right with the world!

— ROBERT BROWNING

Deeply Rooted
The happiness which brings enduring worth to life is not the superficial happiness that is dependent on circumstances. It is the happiness and contentment that fills the soul even in the midst of the most distressing of circumstances and the most bitter environment. It is the kind of happiness that grins when things go wrong and smiles through the tears. The happiness for which our souls ache is one undisturbed by success or failure, one which will root deeply inside us and give inward relaxation, peace, and contentment, no matter what the surface problems may be. That kind of happiness stands in need of no outward stimulus.

— BILLY GRAHAM

One of the sanest, surest, and most generous joys of life comes from being happy over the good fortune of others.

— ARCHIBALD RUTLEDGE

Such happiness as life is capable of comes from the full participation of all our powers in the endeavor to wrest from each changing situation or experience its own full and unique meaning.

— JOHN DEWEY

The inner half of every cloud
   Is bright and shining;
I therefore turn my clouds about,
And always wear them inside out
   To show the lining.

— ELLEN THORNEYCROFT FOWLER

Happiness is not a possession to be prized, it is a quality of thought, a state of mind.

— DAPHNE DU MAURIER

I accept life unconditionally. Life holds so much — so much to be so happy about always. Most people ask for happiness on condition. Happiness can be felt only if you don't set conditions.

— ARTUR RUBINSTEIN

The happiest moments in my life have been the few which I have passed at home in the bosom of my family.

— THOMAS JEFFERSON

Happiness is the full use of your powers along lines of excellence in a life affording scope.

— JOHN F. KENNEDY

There are eight requisites for contented living: health enough to make work a pleasure; wealth enough to support your needs; strength to battle with difficulties and overcome them; grace enough to confess your sins and forsake them; patience enough to toil until some good is accomplished; charity enough to see some good in your neighbor; faith enough to make real the things of God; hope enough to remove all anxious fear concerning the future.

— JOHANN WOLFGANG
VON GOETHE

The best position is one of noninterference with another's peculiar ways of being happy, provided those ways do not interfere by violence with yours.

— WILLIAM JAMES

The measure of a happy life is not from the fewer or more suns we behold, the fewer or more breaths we draw, or meals we repeat, but from having once lived well, acted our part handsomely, and made our exit cheerfully.

— LORD SHAFTESBURY

Helpfulness

They might not need me; but they might.
I'll let my head be just in sight;
A smile as small as mine might be
Precisely their necessity.

Emily Dickinson

You will find, as you look back upon your life, that the moments that stand out are the moments when you have done things for others.

— HENRY DRUMMOND

◆

Helping others, that's the main thing. The only way for us to help ourselves is to help others and to listen to each other's stories.

— ELI WIESEL

◆

Our Common Nature
No one is so rich that he does not need another's help; no one so poor as not to be useful in some way to his fellow man; and the disposition to ask assistance from others with confidence, and to grant it with kindness, is part of our very nature.

— POPE LEO XIII

◆

If I can stop one Heart from breaking,
I shall not live in vain;
If I can ease one Life the Aching,
Or cool one pain,
Or help one fainting Robin
Unto his Nest again,
I shall not live in vain.

— EMILY DICKINSON

There is hunger for ordinary bread, and there is hunger for love, for kindness, for thoughtfulness; and this is the great poverty that makes people suffer so much.

— MOTHER TERESA

◆

After Benjamin Franklin had received a letter thanking him for having done a kindness, he replied: "As to the kindness you mention, I wish I could have been of more service to you than I have been, but if I had, the only thanks that I should desire are that you would always be ready to serve any other person that may need your assistance, and so let good offices go around, for mankind are all of a family. As for my own part, when I am employed in serving others I do not look upon myself as conferring favors but paying debts."

◆

On that best portion of a good man's
	life,
His little, nameless, unremembered acts
Of kindness and of love.

— WILLIAM WORDSWORTH

◆

The only ones among you who will be really happy are those who will have sought and found how to serve.

— ALBERT SCHWEITZER

It is better to light a candle than to curse the darkness.

♦

Working Capital

Open your eyes and look for a human being, or some work devoted to human welfare, which needs from someone a little time or friendliness, a little sympathy, or sociability, or labor. There may be a solitary or an embittered fellow-man, an invalid, or an inefficient person to whom you can be something. Perhaps it is an old person or a child. Or some good work needs volunteers who can offer a free evening, or run errands. Who can enumerate the many ways in which that costly piece of working capital, a human being, can be employed? More of him is wanted everywhere! Search, then, for some investment for your humanity, and do not be frightened away if you have to wait, or to be taken on trial. And be prepared for disappointments. But in any case, do not be without some secondary work in which you can give yourself as a man to men. It is marked out for you, if you only truly will to have it.

— ALBERT SCHWEITZER

♦

It is not so much our friends' help that helps us as the confidence of their help.

— EPICURUS

When I pray, I never pray for myself, always for others, or else I hold a silly, naive, or deadly serious dialogue with what is deepest inside me, which for the sake of convenience I call God. Praying to God for something for yourself strikes me as being too childish for words. To pray for another's well-being is something I find childish as well; one should only pray that another should have enough strength to shoulder his burden. If you do that, you lend him some of your own strength.

— ETTY HILLESUM

♦

I shall not pass this way again;
Then let me now relieve some pain,
Remove some barrier from the road,
Or brighten some one's heavy load.

— EVA ROSE YORK

♦

We who lived in concentration camps can remember the men who walked through the huts comforting others, giving away their last piece of bread. They may have been few in number, but they offer sufficient proof that everything can be taken away from a man but one thing: the last of the human freedoms — to choose one's attitude in any given set of circumstances, to choose one's own way.

— VIKTOR FRANKL

The grass is not, in fact, always greener
on the other side of the fence. Fences
have nothing to do with it. The grass is
greenest where it is watered.

— ROBERT FULGHUM

♦

The best cure for worry, depression,
melancholy, brooding, is to go deliberately forth and try to lift with one's
sympathy the gloom of somebody else.

— ARNOLD BENNETT

♦

A house is built of logs and stone,
  Of tiles and posts and piers;
A home is built of loving deeds
  That stand a thousand years.

— VICTOR HUGO

♦

Die when I may, I want it said of me by
those who knew me best, that I always
plucked a thistle and planted a flower
where I thought a flower would grow.

— ABRAHAM LINCOLN

♦

So long as you wear this mortal body,
you will be subject to weariness and sadness of heart. . . . When this happens,
you will be wise to resort to humble,
exterior tasks, and to restore yourself
by good works.

— THOMAS À KEMPIS

Let us make one point . . . that we meet
each other with a smile, when it is difficult to smile. . . . Smile at each other,
make time for each other in your family.

— MOTHER TERESA

♦

A hundred times every day I remind
myself that my inner and outer life depend on the labors of other men, living
and dead, and that I must exert myself
in order to give in the same measure as
I have received and am still receiving.

— ALBERT EINSTEIN

♦

I sought to hear the
    voice of God
And climbed the
    topmost steeple,
But God declared:
  "Go down again—
I dwell among
    the people."

— JOHN HENRY NEWMAN

♦

In the face of suffering, one has no right
to turn away, not to see. In the face of
injustice, one may not look the other
way. When someone suffers, and it is not
you, he comes first. His very suffering
gives him priority.

— ELI WIESEL

Hope

If you have built castles in the air
Your work need not be lost;
that is where they should be.
Now put foundations under them.

Henry David Thoreau

Everything that is done in the world is done by hope.

— MARTIN LUTHER

♦

The natural flights of the human mind are not from pleasure to pleasure, but from hope to hope.

— SAMUEL JOHNSON

♦

Outreaching Desire
Hope is outreaching desire with expectancy of good. It is a characteristic of all living beings. Birds, beasts, and men are always alert and striving for the fulfillment of their hungers. They are impelled forward in a ceaseless quest for satisfaction. The antennae of insects restlessly explore and feel their way ahead, and the imagination of man functions in the same manner, ranging through wide areas and far futures in search of the good which hope ever promises.

— EDWARD S. AMES

♦

Tomorrow is the most important thing in life. Comes to us at midnight very clean. It's perfect when it arrives and puts itself in our hands. It hopes we've learned something from yesterday.

— JOHN WAYNE

Safekeeping
Do not look forward to the changes and chances of this life in fear; rather look to them with full hope that, as they arise, God, whose you are, will deliver you out of them. He is your keeper. He has kept you hitherto. Do you but hold fast to his dear hand, and he will lead you safely through all things; and, when you cannot stand, he will bear you in his arms. Do not look forward to what may happen tomorrow. Our Father will either shield you from suffering, or he will give you strength to bear it.

— ST. FRANCIS OF SALES

♦

An optimist is the human personification of spring.

— SUSAN J. BISSONETTE

♦

Yet all experience is an arch wherethro'
Gleams that untravell'd world whose
        margin fades
For ever and for ever when I move.

— ALFRED, LORD TENNYSON

♦

Journey to the Stars
If seeds in the black earth can turn into such beautiful roses, what might not the heart of man become in its long journey toward the stars?

— GILBERT KEITH CHESTERTON

If I ascend up into heaven, thou art there: if I make my bed in hell, behold, thou art there.

If I take wings of the morning, and dwell in the uttermost parts of the sea;

Even there shall thy hand lead me, and thy right hand shall hold me.

— PSALM 139:8–10

◆

We stand in life at midnight, we are always on the threshold of a new dawn.

— MARTIN LUTHER KING, JR.

◆

Overhead in an Orchard
Said the Robin to the Sparrow:
"I should really like to know
Why these anxious human beings
Rush about and worry so."

Said the Sparrow to the Robin:
"Friend, I think that it must be
That they have no heavenly Father
Such as cares for you and me."

— ELIZABETH CHENEY

◆

We are haunted by an ideal life, and it is because we have within us the beginning and the possibility of it.

— PHILLIPS BROOKS

Even one's yesterdays could not continue to stir and move in a man's mind unless there were a future for those yesterdays to make.

— MARY ELLEN CHASE

◆

Teacher of Hope
My experience of men has neither disposed me to think worse of them nor indisposed me to serve them; not, in spite of failures which I lament, of errors which I now see and acknowledge, or of the present aspect of affairs, do I despair of the future. The truth is this: The march of Providence is so slow and our desires so impatient; the work of progress is so immense and our means of aiding it so feeble; the life of humanity is so long, that of the individual so brief, that we often see only the ebb of the advancing wave and are thus discouraged. It is history that teaches us to hope.

— ROBERT E. LEE

◆

The longest day must have its close— the gloomiest night will wear on to a morning. An eternal, inexorable lapse of moments is ever hurrying the day of the evil to an eternal night, and the night of the just to an eternal day.

— HARRIET BEECHER STOWE

Man is, properly speaking, based upon hope, he has no other possession but hope; this world of his is emphatically the place of hope.

— THOMAS CARLYLE

♦

Hope—Faith—Love
Nothing that is worth doing can be achieved in our lifetime; therefore we must be saved by hope. Nothing which is true or beautiful or good makes complete sense in any immediate context of history; therefore we must be saved by faith. Nothing we do, however virtuous, can be accomplished alone; therefore we are saved by love. No virtuous act is quite as virtuous from the standpoint of our friend or foe as it is from our standpoint. Therefore we must be saved by the final form of love which is forgiveness.

— REINHOLD NIEBUHR

♦

"Hope" is the thing with feathers—
  That perches in the soul—
And sings the tune without the words—
And never stops—at all.

— EMILY DICKINSON

♦

There are no rules of architecture for a castle in the clouds.

— GILBERT KEITH CHESTERTON

True hope is swift, and flies with
  swallow's wings;
Kings it makes gods, and meaner
  creatures kings.

— WILLIAM SHAKESPEARE

♦

Let us be of good cheer, remembering that the misfortunes hardest to bear are those which never come.

— AMY LOWELL

♦

I have always felt that the moment when you first wake up in the morning is the most wonderful of the twenty-four hours. No matter how weary or dreary you may feel, you possess the certainty that, during the day that lies before you, absolutely anything may happen. And the fact that it practically always *doesn't,* matters not a jot. The possibility is always there.

— MONICA BALDWIN

♦

Our hopes, like towering falcons, aim
At objects in an airy height;
The little pleasure of the game
Is from afar to view the flight.

— MATTHEW PRIOR

♦

Hope springs eternal in the human
  breast;
Man never is, but always to be, blest.

— ALEXANDER POPE

Immortality

I believe in the immortality of the soul because
I have within me immortal longings.

Helen Keller

Immortality

If we really believed that those who are gone from us were as truly alive as ourselves, we could not invest the subject with such awful depth of gloom as we do. If we would imbue our children with distinct faith in immortality, we should never speak of people as dead, but passed into another world. We should speak of the body as a cast-off garment, which the wearer had outgrown; consecrated indeed by the beloved being that used it for a season, but of no value within itself.

—LYDIA MARIA CHILD

♦

I Never Saw a Moor
I never saw a moor,
I never saw the sea;
Yet know I how the heather looks,
And what a wave must be.

I never spoke with God,
Nor visited in heaven;
Yet certain am I of the spot
As if the chart were given.

—EMILY DICKINSON

♦

There is no dark despair that cannot be
Evicted from the heart's Gethsemane;
For faith is always more than unbelief,
And vibrant courage triumphs over
　grief.

—MARY E. MC CULLOUGH

Intimations of Immortality
To every created thing God has given a tongue that proclaims a resurrection. If the Father designs to touch with divine power the cold and pulseless heart of the buried acorn, and make it burst forth from its prison wall, will he leave neglected the soul of man, who is made in the image of his Creator?

If he gives to the rosebush, whose withered blossoms float upon the breeze, the sweet assurance of another springtime, will he withhold the words of hope from the sons of men, when the frosts of winter come?

If matter, mute and inanimate, though changed by the force and nature into a multitude of forms, can never die, will the imperial spirit of man suffer annihilation after a brief sojourn, like a royal guest, in this tenement of clay?

Rather, let us believe that he—who in his apparent prodigality wastes not the raindrop, the blade of grass, or the evening's sighing zephyr, but makes them all to carry out his eternal plan—has given immortality to the mortal!

—WILLIAM JENNINGS BRYAN

♦

One generation passeth away, and another generation cometh: but the earth abideth forever.
The sun also ariseth.

—ECCLESIASTES 1:4–5

Friend

Death is not the enemy of life, but its friend, for it is the knowledge that our years are limited which makes them so precious. It is the truth that time is but lent to us which makes us, at our best, look upon our years as a trust handed into our temporary keeping.

— JOSHUA LOTH LIEBMAN

◆

Each departed friend is a magnet that attracts us to the next world.

— JEAN PAUL RICHTER

◆

The Lord is my shepherd; I shall not want.

He maketh me to lie down in green pastures: he leadeth me beside the still waters.

He restoreth my soul: he leadeth me in the paths of righteousness for his name's sake.

Yea, though I walk through the valley of the shadow of death, I will fear no evil: for thou art with me; thy rod and thy staff they comfort me.

Thou preparest a table before me in the presence of mine enemies: thou anointest my head with oil; my cup runneth over.

Surely goodness and mercy shall follow me all the days of my life: and I will dwell in the house of the Lord for ever.

— PSALM 23

All mankind is of one Author, and is one volume; when one man dies, one chapter is not torn out of the book, but translated into a better language; and every chapter must be so translated; God employs several translators; some pieces are translated by age, some by sickness, some by war, some by justice; but God's hand is in every translation; and his hand shall bind up all our scattered leaves again, for that library where every book shall lie open to one another.

— JOHN DONNE

◆

The bustle in a house
The morning after death
Is solemnest of industries
Enacted upon earth —

The sweeping up the heart,
And putting love away
We shall not want to use again
Until eternity.

— EMILY DICKINSON

◆

The glory of the star, the glory of the sun — we must not lose either in the other. We must not be so full of the hope of heaven that we cannot do our work on the earth; we must not be so lost in the work of the earth that we shall not be inspired by the hope of heaven.

— PHILLIPS BROOKS

Nature

As a fond mother, when the day is o'er,
  Leads by the hand her little child
    to bed,
  Half willing, half reluctant to be led,
  And leave his broken playthings on
    the floor,
Still gazing at them through the open
    door,
  Nor wholly reassured and comforted
  By promises of others in their stead,
  Which, though more splendid, may
    not please him more;
So Nature deals with us, and takes away
  Our playthings one by one, and by
    the hand
  Leads us to rest so gently, that we go
Scarce knowing if we wish to go or stay,
  Being too full of sleep to understand
  How far the unknown transcends the
    what we know.

    — HENRY WADSWORTH
            LONGFELLOW

◆

Life is the childhood of immortality.

    — DANIEL A. POLING

◆

There is, I know not how, in the minds of men, a certain presage, as it were, of a future existence; and this takes the deepest root, and is most discoverable, in the greatest geniuses and most exalted souls.

    — CICERO

Our Creator would never have made such lovely days and have given us the deep hearts to enjoy them, above and beyond all thought, unless we were meant to be immortal.

    — NATHANIEL HAWTHORNE

◆

Eternity is not something that begins after you are dead. It is going on all the time. We are in it now.

    — CHARLOTTE PERKINS GILMAN

◆

The Abiding Love

It singeth low in every heart,
  We hear it each and all, —
A song of those who answer not,
  However we may call;
They throng the silence of the breast,
  We see them as of yore, —
The kind, the brave, the true, the sweet,
  Who walk with us no more.

    — JOHN WHITE CHADWICK

◆

It was not until after the coming of Christ that time and man could breathe freely. It was not until after him that men began to live toward the future. Man does not die in a ditch like a dog — but at home in history, while the work toward the conquest of death is in full swing; he dies sharing in this work.

    — BORIS PASTERNAK

Translation

Our knowledge is but faith moving in
the dark, our joy is a gift of grace, our
immortality a subtle translation of time
into eternity, where all that we have
missed is ours and where what we call
ours is the least part of ourselves. All
belongs to the necessary passion and
death of the spirit, that today rides
upon an ass into its kingdom, to be
crucified tomorrow between two thieves,
and on the third day to rise again from
the dead.

— GEORGE SANTAYANA

◆

Magnificently unprepared
For the long littleness of life.

— FRANCES CORNFORD

◆

What a man believes about immortality
will color his thinking in every area of
life.

— JOHN SUTHERLAND BONNELL

◆

Consolation

He is not dead, this friend; not dead,
But, in the path we mortals tread,
Gone some few, trifling steps ahead,
  And nearer to the end;
So that you, too, once past the bend,
Shall meet again, as face to face, this
  friend
  You fancy dead.

— ROBERT LOUIS STEVENSON

Higher Destiny

We are born for a higher destiny than
that of earth; there is a realm where the
rainbow never fades, where the stars
will be spread before us like islands that
slumber on the ocean, and where the
beings that pass before us like shadows
will stay in our presence forever.

— EDWARD BULWER-LYTTON

◆

The Chariot

Because I could not stop for Death,
He kindly stopped for me;
The carriage held but just ourselves
And Immortality.

We slowly drove, he knew no haste,
And I had put away
My labor, and my leisure too,
For his civility.

We passed the school where children
    played,
Their lessons scarcely done;
We passed the fields of gazing grain,
We passed the setting sun.

We paused before a house that seemed
A swelling on the ground;
The roof was scarcely visible,
The cornice but a mound.

Since then 'tis centuries; but each
Feels shorter than the day
I first surmised the horses' heads
Were toward eternity.

— EMILY DICKINSON

Immortality

from East of Eden

[Liza] looked forward to Heaven as a place where clothes did not get dirty and where food did not have to be cooked and dishes washed. Privately there were some things in Heaven of which she did not quite approve. There was too much singing, and she didn't see how even the Elect could survive for very long the celestial laziness which was promised. She could find something to do in Heaven. There must be something to take up one's time—some clouds to darn, some weary wings to rub with liniment. Maybe the collars of the robes needed turning now and then, and when you come right down to it, she couldn't believe that even in Heaven there would not be cobwebs in some corner to be knocked down with a cloth-covered broom.

— JOHN STEINBECK

♦

Music, when soft voices die,
Vibrates in the memory—
Odors, when sweet violets sicken,
Live within the sense they quicken.

Rose leaves, when the rose is dead,
Are heap'd for the beloved's bed;
And so thy thoughts, when thou art
    gone,
Love itself shall slumber on.

— PERCY BYSSHE SHELLEY

Here in this world He bids us come, there in the next He shall bid us welcome.

— JOHN DONNE

♦

Immortal Symphonies

Winter is on my head but eternal spring is in my heart. The nearer I approach the end, the plainer I hear around me the immortal symphonies of the world to come. For half a century I have been writing my thoughts in prose and verse; but I feel that I have not said one-thousandth part of what is in me. When I have gone down to the grave I shall have ended my day's work; but another day will begin the next morning. Life closes in the twilight but opens with the dawn.

— VICTOR HUGO

♦

Death stands above me, whispering low
  I know not what into my ear;
Of his strange language all I know
  Is, there is not a word of fear.

— WALTER SAVAGE LANDOR

♦

In my Father's house are many mansions; if it were not so, I would have told you. I go to prepare a place for you.

— JOHN 14:2

Influence

I could tell where the lamplighter was
by the trail he left behind him.

Harry Lauder

We are all generals. Whatever action
we take may influence the course of
civilization.

— M. SCOTT PECK

♦

There are two ways of spreading
    light: to be
The candle or the mirror that
    receives it.

— EDITH WHARTON

♦

What People Said

When people talked about Lincoln,
it was nearly always about one or more
of these five things: (1) how long, tall,
quick, strong, or awkward in looks he
was; (2) how he told stories and jokes,
how he was comical or pleasant or
kindly; (3) how he could be silent,
melancholy, sad; (4) how he was ready
to learn and looking for chances to
learn; (5) how he was ready to help
a friend, a stranger, or even a dumb
animal in distress.

— CARL SANDBURG

♦

Do not think it wasted time to submit
yourself to any influence which may
bring upon you any noble feeling.

— JOHN RUSKIN

Living Example

The greatness of Schweitzer—indeed
the essence of Schweitzer—is the man
as symbol. It is not so much what he
has done for others, but what others
have done because of him and the power
of his example. This is the measure of
the man. What has come out of his life
and thought is the kind of inspiration
that can animate a generation. He has
supplied a working demonstration of
reverence for life.

— NORMAN COUSINS

♦

We look into mirrors but we only see
the effects of our times on us—not our
effects on others.

— PEARL BAILEY

♦

Making Life Worthwhile

Every soul that touches yours—
Be it the slightest contact—
Gets therefrom some good;
Some little grace; one kindly thought;
One aspiration yet unfelt;
One bit of courage
For the darkening sky;
One gleam of faith
To brave the thickening ills of life;
One glimpse of brighter skies—
To make this life worthwhile
And heaven a surer heritage.

— GEORGE ELIOT

The world is a looking-glass, and gives back to every man the reflection of his own face. Frown at it, and it in turn will look sourly at you; laugh at it, and with it, and it is a jolly, kind companion.

—WILLIAM MAKEPEACE THACKERAY

♦

One Solitary Life

Here is a man who was born in an obscure village, the child of a peasant woman. He grew up in an obscure village. He worked in a carpenter shop until he was thirty, and then for three years he was an itinerant teacher. He never wrote a book. He never held an office. He never owned a home. He never had a family. He never went to college. He never traveled, except in his infancy, more than two hundred miles from the place where he was born. He never did one of the things that usually accompany greatness. He had no credentials but himself. While he was still a young man, the tide of popular opinion turned against him. His friends ran away. One of them denied him. He was turned over to his enemies. He went through the mockery of a trial. He was nailed upon a cross between two thieves. His executioners gambled for the only piece of property he had on earth, his seamless robe. When he was dead, he was taken down from the cross and laid in a borrowed grave through the courtesy of a friend. Nineteen wide centuries have come and gone, and today he is the centerpiece of the human race and the leader of all human progress. I am well within the mark when I say that all the armies that ever marched, all the navies that ever were built, all the parliaments that ever sat, and all the kings that ever reigned, put together, have not affected the life of man upon this earth as powerfully as has this one solitary personality.

—JAMES A. FRANCIS

♦

There is no power on earth that can neutralize the influence of a high, pure, simple, and useful life.

—BOOKER T. WASHINGTON

♦

Influence

Drop a pebble in the water,
And its ripples reach out far;
And the sunbeams dancing on them
May reflect them to a star.

Give a smile to someone passing,
Thereby making his morning glad;
It may greet you in the evening
When your own heart may be sad.

Do a deed of simple kindness;
Though its end you may not see,
It may reach, like widening ripples,
Down a long eternity.

—JOSEPH NORRIS

Blessed is the influence of one true,
loving soul on another.

— GEORGE ELIOT

♦

An Invisible Host

An American soldier wounded on a
battlefield in the Far East owes his life to
the Japanese scientist Kitasato, who isolated the bacillus of tetanus. A Russian
soldier saved by a blood transfusion is
indebted to Landsteiner, an Austrian. A
German is shielded from typhoid fever
with the help of a Russian, Metchnikoff.
A Dutch marine in the East Indies is
protected from malaria because of the
experiments of an Italian, Grassi; while
a British aviator in North Africa escapes
death from surgical infection because
a Frenchman, Pasteur, and a German,
Koch, elaborated a new technique.

In peace, as in war, we are beneficia-
ries of knowledge contributed by every
nation in the world. Our children are
guarded from diphtheria by what a Japanese and a German did; they are protected from smallpox by the work of an
Englishman; they are saved from rabies
because of a Frenchman; they are cured
of pellagra through the researches of an
Austrian. From birth to death they are
surrounded by an invisible host — the
spirits of men who never thought in
terms of flags or boundary lines and
who never served a lesser loyalty than
the welfare of mankind.

— RAYMOND B. FOSDICK

To Love the Highest

Plutarch's profoundest conviction was
that we needs must love the highest
when we see it — but who can see it
if there are none to show it, first, of
course, in their lives, but, second only to
that, in their words? The one he raised
to a pedestal was the man who made it
easy for people to believe in goodness
and greatness, in heroic courage and
warm generosity and lofty magnanimity.
In humble virtues, too, patience that
never wearies; readiness to forgive; kindness to an erring servant, to an animal.

— EDITH HAMILTON

♦

Shadow-Selves

This learned I from the shadow of
   a tree,
   That to and fro did sway against
    a wall:
   Our shadow-selves, our influence,
   may fall
Where we ourselves can never be.

—ANNA E. HAMILTON

♦

On the whole, ought I not to rejoice
that God was pleased to give me such
a father that from earliest years I had
the example of a real man of God's own
making continually before me? Let me
learn of him. Let me write my books as
he built his houses, and walk as blame-
lessly through this shadow world.

— THOMAS CARLYLE

Joy

Real joy comes not from ease or riches
or from the praise of men, but from
doing something worthwhile.

Wilfred T. Grenfell

Eternal Joy

Eternal joy is the end of the ways of God. The message of all religions is that the Kingdom of God is peace and joy. And it is the message of Christianity. But eternal joy is not to be reached by living on the surface. It is rather attained by breaking through the surface, by penetrating the deep things of ourselves, of our world, and of God. The moment in which we reach the last depth of our lives is the moment in which we can experience the joy that has eternity within it, the hope that cannot be destroyed, and the truth on which life and death are built. For in the depth is truth; and in the depth is hope; and in the depth is joy.

— PAUL TILLICH

To get the full value of joy, you must have someone to divide it with.

— MARK TWAIN

True Joy

This is the true joy in life, the being used for a purpose recognized by yourself as a mighty one; the being thoroughly worn out before you are thrown on the scrap heap; the being a force of Nature instead of a feverish selfish little clod of ailments and grievances complaining that the world will not devote itself to making you happy.

— GEORGE BERNARD SHAW

We have no right to ask when a sorrow comes, "Why did this happen to me?" unless we ask the same question for every joy that comes our way.

— PHILIP F. BERNSTEIN

I certainly wasn't happy. Happiness has to do with reason, and only reason earns it. What I was given was the thing you can't earn, and can't keep, and often don't even recognize at the time; I mean joy.

— URSULA K. LE GUIN

Find joy in simplicity, self-respect, and indifference to what lies between virtue and vice. Love the human race. Follow the divine.

— MARCUS AURELIUS

Join the great company of those who make the barren places of life fruitful with kindness. Carry a vision of heaven in your hearts, and you shall make your name, your college, the world, correspond to that vision. Your success and happiness lie within you. External conditions are the accidents of life, its outer wrappings. The great, enduring realities are love and service. Joy is the holy fire that keeps our purpose warm and our intelligence aglow. Resolve to keep happy, and your joy and you shall form an invincible host against difficulty.

— HELEN KELLER

No Regrets

There is only one thing about which I shall have no regrets when my life ends. I have savored to the full all the small, daily joys. The bright sunshine on the breakfast table; the smell of the air at dusk; the sound of the clock ticking; the light rains that start gently after midnight; the hour when the family come home; Sunday-evening tea before the fire! I have never missed one moment of beauty, not ever taken it for granted. Spring, summer, autumn, or winter. I wish I had failed as little in other ways.

— AGNES SLIGH TURNBULL

♦

Philosophy of Focus

One morning in the throes of a dismal headache I took my pen and sketched a philosophy of focus:

The truth which cannot alter,
The hope that cannot fail,
The faith that cannot falter,
The peace which shall prevail,
The strength which God has
   promised,
The life his love made real,
I leave unto his keeping
Come woe or come weal.

I exchanged the headache for a joyful heart.

— NELS F. S. FERRÉ

Alas for the worn and heavy soul if it has outlived its privilege of springtime and sprightliness.

— NATHANIEL HAWTHORNE

♦

Highest Joy

A new day rose upon me. It was as if another sun had risen into the sky; the heavens were indescribably brighter, and the earth fairer; and that day has gone on brightening to the present hour. I have known the other joys of life, I suppose, as much as most men; I have known art and beauty, music and gladness; I have known friendship and love and family ties; but it is certain that till we see God in the world — God in the bright and boundless universe — we never know the highest joy. It is far more than if one were translated to a world a thousand times fairer than this; for that supreme and central Light of Infinite Love and Wisdom, shining over this world and all worlds, alone can show us how noble and beautiful, how fair and glorious they are.

— ORVILLE DEWEY

♦

I cannot believe that the inscrutable universe turns on an axis of suffering; surely the strange beauty of the world must somewhere rest on pure joy.

— LOUISE BOGAN

Testimony

This is a cheerful world as I see it from my garden under the shadows of my vines. But if I were to ascend some high mountain and look out over the wide lands, you know very well what I should see: brigands on the highways, pirates on the sea, armies fighting, cities burning; in the amphitheaters men murdered to please applauding crowds; selfishness and cruelty and misery and despair under all roofs. It is a bad world, Donatus, an incredibly bad world. But I have discovered in the midst of it a quiet and holy people who have learned a great secret. They have found a joy which is a thousand times better than any pleasure of our sinful life. They are despised and persecuted, but they care not. They are masters of their souls. They have overcome the world. These people, Donatus, are the Christians—and I am one of them.

— ST. CYPRIAN

♦

Alchemy

I lift my heart as spring lifts up
  A yellow daisy to the rain;
My heart wilt be a lovely cup
  Altho' it holds but pain.

For I shall learn from flower and leaf
  That color every drop they hold,
To change the lifeless wine of grief
  To living gold.

— SARA TEASDALE

Eloquence

The hands of those I meet are dumbly eloquent to me. I have met people so empty of joy that when I clasped their frosty fingertips it seemed as if I were shaking hands with a northeast storm. Others there are whose hands have sunbeams in them, so that their grasp warms my heart. It may be only the clinging touch of a child's hand, but there is as much potential sunshine in it for me as there is in a loving glance for others.

— HELEN KELLER

♦

A joyful heart is good medicine, but a broken spirit dries up the bones.

— PROVERBS 17:22

♦

His Coming

He comes to us as one unknown, without a name, as of old by the lakeside he came to those men who knew him not. He speaks to us the same word, "Follow thou me," and sets us to the tasks which he has to fulfill for our time. He commands. And to those who obey, whether they be wise or simple, he will reveal himself in the toils, the conflicts, the suffering which they shall pass through in his fellowship, and as an ineffable mystery, they shall learn in their own experience who he is.

— ALBERT SCHWEITZER

Laughter

He who laughs, lasts.

Mary Pettibone Poole

With the fearful strain that is on me day and night, if I did not laugh, I should die.

—ABRAHAM LINCOLN

Laughter can relieve tension, soothe the pain of disappointment, and strengthen the spirit for the formidable tasks that always lie ahead.

—DWIGHT D. EISENHOWER

Frame your mind to mirth and
   merriment,
Which bars a thousand harms and
   lengthens life.

—WILLIAM SHAKESPEARE

The most wasted of all days is that during which one has not laughed.

—SÉBASTIEN-ROCH
NICOLAS CHAMFORT

Solitude
Laugh and the world laughs with you,
   Weep and you weep alone;
For the sad old earth must borrow its
   mirth,
   But has troubles enough of its own.

—ELLA WHEELER WILCOX

Laughing is the sensation of feeling good all over and showing it principally in one spot.

—JOSH BILLINGS

From quiet homes and first beginning,
Out to the undiscovered ends,
There's nothing worth the wear of
   winning,
But laughter and the love of friends.

—HILAIRE BELLOC

Laughing Song
When the green woods laugh with
   the voice of joy,
And the dimpling stream runs
   laughing by;
When the air does laugh with our
   merry wit,
And the green hill laughs with the
   noise of it.

—WILLIAM BLAKE

Nothing, no experience good or bad, no belief, no cause, is in itself momentous enough to monopolize the whole of life to the exclusion of laughter.

—ALFRED NORTH WHITEHEAD

A good laugh is sunshine in a house.

—WILLIAM MAKEPEACE
THACKERAY

Everything is funny as long as it is
happening to someone else.

— WILL ROGERS

Men have been wise in very different
modes; but they have always laughed
the same way.

— SAMUEL JOHNSON

Ariel
Low gurgling laughter, as sweet
  As the swallow's song i' the South,
And a ripple of dimples that, dancing,
  meet
  By the curves of a perfect mouth.

— PAUL HAMILTON HAYNE

Humor is a prelude to faith and
Laughter is the beginning of prayer.

— REINHOLD NIEBUHR

Man is the only animal that laughs and
weeps; for he is the only animal that is
struck with the difference between what
things are and what they might have
been.

— WILLIAM HAZLITT

Those who do not know how to weep
with their whole heart don't know how
to laugh either.

— GOLDA MEIR

Shared laughter creates a bond of
friendship. When people laugh together,
they cease to be young and old, master
and pupils, worker and driver. They
have become a single group of human
beings, enjoying their existence.

— W. GRANT LEE

For a man learns more quickly and
remembers more easily that which he
laughs at, than that which he approves
and reveres.

— HORACE

We cannot really love anybody with
whom we never laugh.

— AGNES REPPLIER

Knowledge
I have known sorrow — therefore I
May laugh with you, O friend,
  more merrily
Than those who never sorrowed
  upon earth
And know not laughter's worth.

I have known laughter—therefore I
May sorrow with you far more tenderly
Than those who never guess how sad
  a thing
Seems merriment to one heart's
  suffering.

— THEODOSIA GARRISON

We know the degree of refinement in men by the matter they laugh at and by the ring of the laugh.

— GEORGE MEREDITH

We are all here for a spell, get all the good laughs you can.

— WILL ROGERS

A clown may be the first in the kingdom of heaven, if he has helped lessen the sadness of human life.

— RABBI BAROKA

Teach us Delight in simple things,
And Mirth that has no bitter springs;
Forgiveness free of evil done,
And Love to all men 'neath the sun!

— RUDYARD KIPLING

Ode

I am the laughter of the new-born child
On whose soft-breathing sleep an angel
　　smiled.

— R. W. GILDER

The human race has only one effective weapon and that is laughter.

— MARK TWAIN

Nothing shows a man's character more than what he laughs at.

— JOHANN WOLFGANG
VON GOETHE

I am forced to try to make myself laugh that I may not cry: for one or the other I must do; and is it not philosophy carried to the highest pitch for a man to conquer such tumults of soul as I am sometimes agitated by, and in the very height of the storm to quaver out a horselaugh?

— SAMUEL RICHARDSON

The most valuable sense of humor is the kind that enables a person to see instantly what it isn't safe to laugh at.

The young man who has not wept is a savage, and the old man who will not laugh is a fool.

— GEORGE SANTAYANA

All people that on earth do dwell,
Sing to the Lord with cheerful voice.
Him serve with mirth, his praise
　　forth tell,
Come ye before him and rejoice.

— WILLIAM KETHE
(attrib.)

Life

God asks no man whether he will accept life.
That is not the choice.
You must take it.
The only choice is how.

Henry Ward Beecher

Life is a pure flame, and we live by an invisible sun within us.

— THOMAS BROWNE

♦

The year hastens to a close. What is it to me? What am I, that all that affects me? That I am twenty-eight or eighty or fifty-eight years old is nothing. Should I mourn that the spring flowers are gone, that the summer fruit has ripened, that the harvest is reaped, that the snow has fallen?

— RALPH WALDO EMERSON
(journal entry, 28 December 1831; age 28)

♦

People who fight fire with fire usually end up with ashes.

— ABIGAIL VAN BUREN

♦

No one imagines that a symphony is supposed to improve in quality as it goes along, or that the whole object of playing it is to reach the finale. The point of music is discovered in every moment of playing and listening to it. It is the same, I feel, with the greater part of our lives, and if we are unduly absorbed in improving them we may forget altogether to live them.

— ALAN WATTS

Man's Life
The life of man seems to me like the flight of a sparrow through the hall wherein you are sitting at supper in the winter time, a warm fire lighted on the hearth while storms rage without. The sparrow flies in at one door, tarries for a moment in the light and heat, and then flying forth through another door vanishes into the wintry darkness whence it had come. So tarries man for a brief space, but of what went before or what is to follow, we know not.

— THE VENERABLE BEDE

♦

Be not afraid of life. Believe that life is worth living, and your belief will help create the fact.

— WILLIAM JAMES

♦

How could one have wished him a happier death? He dies almost unconsciously in the fullness of success, and martyrdom in so great a cause consecrates his name through all history. Such a death is the crown of a noble life.

— JOHN STUART MILL
(on Lincoln)

Voyage

Think of life as a voyage. The truest
liver of the truest life is like a voyager
who, as he sails, is not indifferent to
all the beauty of the sea around him.
The morning and the evening sun, the
moonlight and the starlight, the endless
change of the vast water that he floats
on, the passing back and forth of other
ships between him and the sky, the
incidents and company on his own
vessel — all these are pleasant to him; but
their pleasure is borne up by and woven
in with his interest in the purpose for
which he undertook the voyage. That
lies beyond and that lies under the voyage all the while. He is not sailing just
for the sake of sailing. He would never
have undertaken the voyage for his own
sake. Another man, who has no purpose
beyond the voyage, is vexed and uneasy.
He is so afraid of not getting the best
out of it that he loses its best. The spots
and imperfections in its pleasure worry
him. Those are the differences of the
ways in which men live. One man for-
gets his own life in the purposes for
which his life is lived, and he is the man
whose life grows richest and brightest.
Another man is always thinking about
himself, and so never gets beyond himself into those purposes of living out of
which all the fullness of personal life
may flow back to him.

— PHILLIPS BROOKS

The more we live, more brief appears
Our life's succeeding stages
A day to childhood seems a year
And years like passing ages.

— THOMAS CAMPBELL

◆

The great use of life is to spend it for
something that outlasts it.

— WILLIAM JAMES

◆

It does not astonish or make us angry
that it takes a whole year to bring into
the house three great white peonies and
two pale blue iris. It seems altogether
right and appropriate that these glories
are earned with long patience and faith.
. . . and also that it is altogether right
and appropriate that they cannot last.
Yet in our human relations we are out-
raged when the supreme moments, the
moments of flowering, must be waited
for . . . and then cannot *last*. We reach
a summit, and then have to go down
again.

— MAY SARTON

◆

Living is a form of not being sure, not
knowing what next or how.

— AGNES DE MILLE

All of my past life that has not faded into the mist has passed through the filter, not of my mind, but of my affections.

— IRIS ORIGO

♦

To laugh often and much; to win the respect of intelligent people and the affection of children; to earn the appreciation of honest criticism and endure the betrayal of false friends; to appreciate beauty and find the best in others; to leave this world a bit better whether by a healthy child, a garden patch, a redeemed social condition; to know even one life has breathed easier because you have lived — this is to have succeeded.

— RALPH WALDO EMERSON

♦

Nothing seems so tragic to one who is old as the death of one who is young, and this alone proves that life is a good thing.

— ZOE ATKINS

♦

from Death of an Expert Witness
It was not . . . that she was unaware of the frayed and ragged edges of life. She would merely iron them out with a firm hand and neatly hem them down.

— P. D. JAMES

How—When—Where
It is not so much WHERE you live,
As HOW, and WHY, and WHEN you live,
That answers in the affirmative,
Or maybe in the negative,
The question — Are you fit to live?

It is not so much WHERE you live,
As HOW you live, and whether good
Flows from you through your
    neighborhood.

And WHY you live, and whether you
Aim high and noblest ends pursue,
And keep Life brimming full and true.

And WHEN you live, and whether Time
Is at its nadir or its prime,
And whether you descend or climb.

It is not so much WHERE you live,
As whether while you live you *live*
And to the world your highest give,
And so make answer positive
That you are truly fit to live.

— JOHN OXENHAM

♦

Life offstage has sometimes been a wilderness of unpredictables in an unchoreographed world.

— MARGOT FONTEYN

♦

Do not seek death. Death will find you. But seek the road which makes death a fulfillment.

— DAG HAMMARSKJÖLD

The end is nothing; the road is all.

— WILLA CATHER

◆

I believe that man will not merely endure: he will prevail. He is immortal,
not because he alone among creatures
has an inexhaustible voice, but because
he has a soul, a spirit capable of compassion and sacrifice and endurance.

— WILLIAM FAULKNER

◆

How vain it is to sit down to write if
you have not stood up to live.

— HENRY DAVID THOREAU

◆

The Winds of Fate
One ship drives east and another
    drives west
  With the selfsame winds that
    blow.
    'Tis the set of the sails
    And not the gales
  Which tells us the way to go.

Like the winds of the sea are the
    ways of fate,
  As we voyage along through life:
    'Tis the set of a soul
    That decides its goal,
  And not the calm or the strife.

— ELLA WHEELER WILCOX

Grammar
Live in the active voice, rather than in
  the passive. Think more about what
  you make happen than what is happening to you.
Live in the indicative mood, rather than
  in the subjunctive. Be concerned
  with things as they are, rather than
  as they might be.
Live in the present tense, facing the duty
  at hand without regret for the past
  or worry over the future.
Live in the singular number, caring
  more for the approval of your own
  conscience than for the applause of
  the crowd.

— WILLIAM DE WITT HYDE

◆

Life is difficult. This is a great truth,
one of the greatest truths. It is a great
truth because once we truly see this
truth, we transcend it. Once we truly
know that life is difficult — once we truly
understand and accept it — then life is
no longer difficult. Because once it is
accepted, the fact that life is difficult
no longer matters.

— M. SCOTT PECK

◆

I'd decided that I would make my life
my argument. I would advocate the
things I believed in terms of the life
I lived and what I did.

— ALBERT SCHWEITZER

Listen to your life. See it for the fathomless mystery that it is. In the boredom and pain of it no less than in the excitement and gladness: touch, taste, smell your way to the holy and hidden heart of it because in the last analysis all moments are key moments, and life itself is grace.

— FREDERICK BUECHNER

◆

Life is a series of surprises, and would not be worth taking or keeping if it were not.

— RALPH WALDO EMERSON

◆

For a Contented Life

Health enough to make work a
    pleasure.
Wealth enough to support your needs.
Strength to battle with difficulties and
    overcome them.
Grace enough to confess your sins and
    forsake them.
Patience enough to toil until some
    good is accomplished.
Charity enough to see some good in
    your neighbor.
Love enough to move you to be useful
    and helpful to others.
Faith enough to make real the things
    of God.
Hope enough to remove all anxious
    fears concerning the future.

— JOHANN WOLFGANG
VON GOETHE

When we were children we used to think that when we were grown-up we would no longer be vulnerable. But to grow up is to accept vulnerability. . . . To be alive is to be vulnerable.

— MADELEINE L'ENGLE

◆

The way through the world is more difficult to find than the way around it.

— WALLACE STEVENS

◆

Life is no brief candle to me. It is a sort of splendid torch which I have got hold of for the moment, and I want to make it burn as brightly as possible before handing it on to future generations.

— GEORGE BERNARD SHAW

◆

Tadpole into frog, sketch into statue . . . — evolution is fascinating to watch. To me it is most interesting when one observes the evolution of a single man.

— SHANA ALEXANDER

◆

Life is either a daring adventure or nothing. To keep our faces toward change and behave like free spirits in the presence of fate is strength undefeatable.

— HELEN KELLER

Love

Love cannot be forced,
love cannot be coaxed and teased.
It comes out of Heaven,
unasked and unsought.

Pearl Buck

The Eskimos had fifty-two names for snow because snow was important to them: there ought to be as many for love.

— MARGARET ATWOOD

♦

Love is something eternal — the aspect may change, but not the essence. There is the same difference in a person before and after he is in love as there is in an unlighted lamp and one that is burning. The lamp was there and it was a good lamp, but now it is shedding light, too, and that is its real function.

— VINCENT VAN GOGH

♦

When I was one-and-twenty
  I heard a wise man say,
"Give crowns and pounds and
    guineas,
  But not your heart away;
Give pearls away and rubies
  But keep your fancy free!"
But I was one-and-twenty,
  No use to talk to me.

When I was one-and-twenty
  I heard him say again,
"The heart out of the bosom
  Was never given in vain;
'Tis paid with sighs a plenty
  And sold for endless rue."
And I am two-and-twenty,
  And oh, 'tis true, 'tis true.

— A. E. HOUSMAN

The Love of God

There is an ocean — cold water without motion. In this ocean, however, is the Gulf Stream, hot water flowing from the equator toward the Pole. Inquire of all scientists how it is physically imaginable that a stream of hot water flows between the waters of the ocean, which, so to speak, form its banks, the moving within the motionless, the hot within the cold. No scientist can explain it. Similarly, there is the God of love within the God of the forces of the universe — one with him, and yet so totally different. We let ourselves be seized and carried away by that vital stream.

— ALBERT SCHWEITZER

♦

Second Sowing

There is no harvest for the heart alone;
The seed of love must be
Eternally
Resown.

— ANNE MORROW LINDBERGH

♦

The first element of greatness is fundamental humbleness (this should not be confused with servility); the second is freedom from self; the third is intrepid courage, which, taken in its widest interpretation, generally goes with truth; and the fourth — the power of love — although I have put it last, is the rarest.

— MARGOT ASQUITH

All-Embracing Love

Love all God's creation, both the whole and every grain of sand. Love every leaf, every ray of light. Love the animals, love the plants, love each separate thing. If thou love each thing thou will perceive the mystery of God in all; and when once thou perceive this, thou wilt thenceforward grow every day to a fuller understanding of it: until thou come at last to love the whole world with a love that will then be all-embracing and universal.

— FYODOR DOSTOEVSKI

♦

'Tis better to have loved and lost
Than never to have loved at all.

— ALFRED, LORD TENNYSON

♦

For a Wedding Anniversary

Companioned years have made them
  comprehend
The comradeship that lies beyond a kiss.
The young ask much of life — they ask
  but this,
To fare the road together to its end.

— ROSELLE MERCIER MONTGOMERY

♦

I like not only to be loved, but to be told that I am loved; the realm of silence is large enough beyond the grave.

— GEORGE ELIOT

We never live so intensely as when we love strongly. We never realize ourselves so vividly as when we are in the full glow of love for others.

— WALTER RAUSCHENBUSCH

♦

Though I speak with the tongues of men and of angels, and have not love, I am become as sounding brass or a tinkling cymbal.

And though I have the gift of prophecy, and understand all mysteries, and all knowledge; and though I have all faith, so that I could remove mountains, and have not love, I am nothing.

— I CORINTHIANS 13:1–2

♦

To love is to know the sacrifices that eternity extracts from life.

— PEARL CRAIGIE

♦

"Thou shalt love the Lord thy God with thy whole heart, with thy whole soul, and with thy whole mind." This is the commandment of the great God, and He cannot command the impossible. Love is a fruit in season at all times, and within reach of every hand. Anyone may gather it and no limit is set. Everyone can reach this love through meditation, spirit of prayer, and sacrifice, by an intense inner life.

— MOTHER TERESA

Season of Love

We miss the spirit of Christmas if we
consider the incarnation as an indistinct
and doubtful, far-off event unrelated
to our present problems. We miss the
purport of Christ's birth if we do not
accept it as a living link which joins us
together in spirit as children of the ever-
living and true God. In love alone —
the love of God and the love of man —
will be found the solution of all the ills
which afflict the world today. Slowly,
sometimes painfully, but always with
increasing purpose, emerges the great
message of Christianity: Only with
wisdom comes joy, and with greatness
comes love.

— HARRY S. TRUMAN

♦

I define love thus: The will to extend
one's self for the purpose of nurturing
one's own or another's spiritual growth.

— M. SCOTT PECK

♦

The bottom line is that (a) people are
never perfect, but love can be, (b) that is
the one and only way that the mediocre
and the vile can be transformed, and (c)
doing that makes it that. We waste time
looking for the perfect lover, instead of
creating the perfect love.

— TOM ROBBINS

He loves each one of us, as if there were
only one of us.

— ST. AUGUSTINE

♦

How do I love thee? Let me count the
    ways.
I love thee to the depth and breadth
    and height
My soul can reach, when feeling out
    of sight
For the ends of Being and ideal Grace.
I love thee to the level of everyday's
Most quiet need, by sun and candle-
    light.
I love thee freely, as men strive for
    Right;
I love thee purely, as they turn from
    Praise.
I love thee with the passion put to use
In my old griefs, and with my
    childhood's faith.
I love thee with a love I seemed to lose
With my lost saints, — I love thee with
    the breath,
Smiles, tears, of all my life! — and, if
    God choose,
I shall but love thee better after death.

— ELIZABETH BARRETT BROWNING

♦

Go often to the house of thy friend, for
weeds choke the unused path.

— RALPH WALDO EMERSON

Love doesn't just sit there like a stone, it has to be made, like bread; re-made all the time, made new.

—URSULA K. LE GUIN

Love is never lost. If not reciprocated, it will flow back and soften and purify the heart.

—WASHINGTON IRVING

Prayer at Eventide
This day is almost done. When the night and morning meet it will be only an unalterable memory. So let no unkind word, no careless doubting thought, no guilty secret, no neglected duty, no wisp or jealous fog becloud its passing. Now, in token of our deep and abiding love, we would lay aside all disturbing thoughts, all misunderstandings, all unworthiness. If things have gone awry, let neither of us lift an accusing finger. Who is to blame is not important; only how shall we set the situation right. And so, serving and being served, loving and being loved, we shall make a peaceful home, where we and our children shall learn to face life joyfully, triumphantly, so near as God shall give us grace.

—F. ALEXANDER MAGOUN

Many waters cannot quench love, neither can the floods drown it.

—SONG OF SOLOMON 8:7

Learning to Love
There are many who want me to tell them of secret ways of becoming perfect and I can only tell them that the sole secret is a hearty love of God, and the only way of attaining that love is by loving. You learn to speak by speaking, to study by studying, to run by running, to work by working; and just so you learn to love God and man by loving. Begin as a mere apprentice and the very power of love will lead you on to become a master of the art.

—ST. FRANCIS OF SALES

The kindest and the happiest pair
Will find occasion to forbear;
And something, every day they live,
To pity, and perhaps forgive

—WILLIAM COWPER

Love does not consist in gazing at each other, but in looking outward together in the same direction.

—ANTOINE DE SAINT-EXUPÉRY

A Child Learns About Love

I remember the morning that I first asked the meaning of the word "love." This was before I knew many words. I had found a few early violets in the garden and brought them to my teacher. She tried to kiss me; but at that time I did not like to have anyone kiss me except my mother. Miss Sullivan put her arm gently round me and spelled into my hand, "I love Helen."

"What is love?" I asked.

She drew me closer to her and said, "It is here," pointing to my heart. . . . Her words puzzled me very much because I did not then understand anything unless I touched it.

I smelled the violets in her hand and asked, half in words, half in signs, a question which meant, "Is love the sweetness of flowers?"

"No," said my teacher.

Again I thought. The warm sun was shining on us.

"Is this not love?" I asked, pointing in the direction from which the heat came. . . .

A day or two afterward . . . the sun had been under a cloud all day, and there had been brief showers, but suddenly the sun broke forth in all its southern splendor. Again I asked my teacher, "Is this not love?"

"Love is something like the clouds that were in the sky before the sun came out," she replied. Then in simpler words than these, which at that time I could not have understood, she explained: "You cannot touch the clouds, you know; but you feel the rain and know how glad the flowers and the thirsty earth are to have it after a hot day. You cannot touch love either; but you feel the sweetness that it pours into everything. Without love you would not be happy or want to play."

The beautiful truth burst upon my mind—I felt that these were invisible lines stretched between my spirit and the spirits of others.

—HELEN KELLER

Nature

Earth's crammed with heaven,
And every common bush afire with God.

Elizabeth Barrett Browning

Nature is the living, visible garment
of God.

— JOHANN WOLFGANG
VON GOETHE

There were few sounds that night except those of the water and the water
birds. The wind was asleep. From the
direction of the inlet there came the
sound of breakers on the barrier beach,
but the distant voice of the sea was
hushed almost to a sigh, a sort of rhythmic exhalation as though the sea, too,
were asleep outside the gates of the
sound.

It would have taken the sharpest ears
to catch the sound of a hermit crab dragging his shell house along the beach just
above the water line: the elfin shuffle of
his feet on the sand, the sharp grit as he
dragged his own shell across another; or
to have discerned the spattering tinkle
of the tiny droplets that fell when a
shrimp, being pursued by a school of
fish, leaped clear of the water. But these
were the unheard voices of the island
night, of the water and the water's edge.

— RACHEL CARSON

I believe that there is a subtle magnetism
in Nature, which, if we unconsciously
yield to it, will direct us aright.

— HENRY DAVID THOREAU

The beauty of the trees,
the softness of the air,
the fragrance of the grass,
  speaks to me.

The summit of the mountain,
the thunder of the sky,
the rhythm of the sea,
  speaks to me.

The faintness of the stars,
the freshness of the morning,
the dewdrop on the flower,
  speaks to me.

The strength of fire,
the taste of salmon,
the trail of the sun,
and the life that never goes away,
  they speak to me.

And my heart soars.

— CHIEF DAN GEORGE

The garden is growth and change and
that means loss as well as constant new
treasures to make up for a few disasters.

— MAY SARTON

Beauty is pervasive, and fills, like
perfume, more than the object that
contains it. Because I had known
intimately a river, the earth pulsed
under me.

— MARJORIE KINNAN RAWLINGS

I go now to the wilderness to be a part of it; to accept my place in the world and its place in me; to grow into reality as a tree grows into the rain, to conform to the Earth as a stream conforms to the stones of its bed. To live. To aspire. To be.

— WILLIAM ASHWORTH

•

Some keep the Sabbath going to church;
I keep it staying at home,
With a bobolink for a chorister,
And an orchard for a dome.

Some keep the Sabbath in surplice;
I just wear my wings,
And instead of tolling the bell for
    church,
Our little sexton sings.

God preaches, — a noted clergyman, —
And the sermon is never long;
So instead of getting to heaven at last,
I'm going all along!

— EMILY DICKINSON

•

If spring came but once in a century instead of once a year, or burst forth with the sound of an earthquake and not in silence, what wonder and expectation there would be in all hearts to behold the miraculous change.

— HENRY WADSWORTH
LONGFELLOW

This is a snail shell, round, full and glossy as a horse chestnut. Comfortable and compact, it sits curled up like a cat in the hollow of my hand. Milky and opaque, it has the pinkish bloom of the sky on a summer evening, ripening to rain. On its smooth symmetrical face is pencilled with precision a perfect spiral, winding inward to the pinpoint center of the shell, the tiny dark core of the apex, the pupil of the eye. It stares at me, this mysterious single eye — and I stare back.

— ANNE MORROW LINDBERGH

•

Rightly considered, modern scientific development gives us a profound conception of God because it gives us a better idea than heretofore of the inexhaustible activity of God. In enlarging indefinitely the limits of the universe created by God, we have enlarged our understanding of the Creator's power.

— J. ELLIOTT ROSS

•

I love to think of nature as an unlimited broadcasting station, through which God speaks to us every hour, if we will only tune in.

— GEORGE WASHINGTON CARVER

On Wistman's Wood

The place has an immense stillness, as if
here the plant side of creation rules and
even birds are banned; below, through
the intricate green gladelets and branch-
gardens, comes the rush of water in a
moorland stream. . . . This water-noise,
like the snore of the raven, the breeding-
trill of the distant curlew, seems to come
from another world.

— JOHN FOWLES

♦

In every outthrust headland, in every
curving beach, in every grain of sand
there is a story of the earth.

— RACHEL CARSON

♦

Kepler stood before his telescope, view-
ing the star clusters of a night sky, and
cried out, "O God, I think thy thoughts
after thee."

♦

Climb the mountains and get good tid-
ings. Nature's peace will flow into you as
sunshine flows into trees. The winds will
blow their own freshness into you, and
the storms their energy, while cares will
drop away from you like the leaves of
Autumn.

— JOHN MUIR

Nature teaches beasts to know their
friends.

— WILLIAM SHAKESPEARE

♦

The earth is at the same time mother,
she is mother of all that is natural,
    mother of all that is human,
She is the mother of all,
for contained in her
are the seeds of all.

The earth of humankind
contains all moistness,
    all verdancy,
    all germinating power.

It is in so many ways fruitful.
All creation comes from it.
Yet it forms not only the basic
raw material for humankind,
but also the substance
of the incarnation
of God's son.

— HILDEGARD OF BINGEN

♦

Flower in the crannied wall,
I pluck you out of the crannies,
I hold you, root and all, in my hand,
Little flower—but *if* I could understand
What you are, root and all, and all in all,
I should know what God and man is.

— ALFRED, LORD TENNYSON

Opportunity

The lure of the distant
and the difficult is deceptive.
The great opportunity is where you are.

John Burroughs

The Tide

There is a tide in the affairs of men
Which taken at the flood, leads on to
    fortune;
Omitted, all the voyage of their life,
Is bound in shallows and in miseries.

— WILLIAM SHAKESPEARE

♦

The Little Task

Always keep your eyes open for the little
task, because it is the little task that is
important to Jesus Christ. The future of
the Kingdom of God does not depend
on the enthusiasm of this or that powerful person; those great ones are necessary
too, but it is equally necessary to have
a great number of little people who will
do a little thing in the service of Christ.
The great flowing rivers represent only
a small part of all the water that is necessary to nourish and sustain the earth.
Beside the flowing river there is the
water in the earth—the subterranean
water—and there are the little streams
which continually enter the river and
feed it and prevent it from sinking into
the earth. Without these other waters—
the silent hidden subterranean waters
and the trickling streams—the great
river could no longer flow. Thus it is
with the little tasks to be fulfilled by
us all.

— ALBERT SCHWEITZER

Every great mistake has a halfway
moment, a split second when it can
be recalled and perhaps remedied.

— PEARL S. BUCK

♦

That best picture has not yet been
painted; the greatest poem is still un-
sung; the mightiest novel remains to
be written; the divinest music has not
been conceived even by Bach. In science,
probably ninety-nine percent of the
knowable has not yet been discovered.

— LINCOLN STEFFENS

♦

Make the most of the best and the least
of the worst.

— ROBERT LOUIS STEVENSON

♦

Lost yesterday, somewhere between
sunrise and sunset, two golden hours,
each set with sixty diamond minutes.
No reward is offered, for they are gone
forever.

— HORACE MANN

♦

from The Road Not Taken

I shall be telling this with a sigh
Somewhere ages and ages hence;
Two roads diverged in a wood, and I,
I took the one less traveled by—
And that has made all the difference.

— ROBERT FROST

Sculpturing

It is something to be able to paint a
particular picture, or to carve a statue,
and so to make a few objects beautiful;
but it is far more glorious to carve and
paint the very atmosphere and medium
through which we look. To affect the
quality of the day—that is the highest
of arts.

— HENRY DAVID THOREAU

♦

The hardest thing to believe when
you're young is that people will fight to
stay in a rut, but not to get out of one.

— ELLEN GLASGOW

♦

Days

Daughters of Time, the hypocritic Days,
Muffled and dumb like barefoot
    dervishes,
And marching single in an endless file,
Bring diadems and fagots in their hands.
To each they offer gifts after his will,
Bread, kingdom, stars, and sky that
    holds them all.
I, in my pleached garden, watched
    the pomp,
Forgot my morning wishes, hastily
Took a few herbs and apples, and
    the Day
Turned and departed silent. I, too late,
Under her solemn filet saw the scorn.

— RALPH WALDO EMERSON

Enlargement

The night sky does something to the
star-gazer. There is silent, uplifting inspiration from the Absolute. It does us
creative good to look up and "see Orion
driving his hunting dogs across the
Zenith or Andromeda shaking out her
tresses over limitless space." It enlarges
the self to know great art, to have studied great architecture, to have felt the
spell of epic heroisms, to have swung to
the rhythmic pulse of Homer's strophes,
to have shaken to the passion of Roland,
or Romeo, or Francis of Assisi, to have
wrestled with Kant's categorical impera-
tives, to have seen the twin-flower in
Linnaeus' companionship, to have
heard the roll of Drake's drum, to have
been borne on the music stream of
Beethoven's symphonies, to engrave the
prologue to John's Gospel on the heart,
to have said the sonorous, searching
affirmations of the Nicene Creed.

— PHILLIPS ENDICOTT OSGOOD

♦

The price of liberty is eternal vigilance.

— FREDERICK DOUGLASS

♦

When written in Chinese, the word
"crisis" is composed of two characters—
one represents danger and the other
represents opportunity.

— JOHN F. KENNEDY

Go seeker, if you will, throughout the land. . . . Observe the whole of it, survey as you might survey a field. . . . It's your oyster — yours to open if you will. . . . Just make yourself at home, refresh yourself, get the feel of things, adjust your sights, and get the scale. . . . To every man his chance — to man, regardless of birth, his shining, golden opportunity — to every man the right to live, to work, to be himself, to become whatever thing his manhood and his vision can combine to make him — this, seeker, is the promise of America.

— THOMAS WOLFE

♦

We must use time creatively . . . and forever realize that the time is always ripe to do right.

— MARTIN LUTHER KING, JR.

♦

Faith is the hinge that opens the door to opportunity.

— JOHN HUNTER

♦

In the modern world of business, it is useless to be a creative original thinker unless you can also sell what you create. Management cannot be expected to recognize a good idea unless it is presented to them by a good salesman.

— DAVID M. OGILVY

The pessimist sees the difficulty in every opportunity; the optimist, the opportunity in every difficulty.

— L. P. JACKS

♦

When one door is shut, another opens.

— CERVANTES

♦

We need you, we need your youth, your strength, and your idealism, to help us make right that which is wrong. I know you have been critically looking at the mores and customs of the past and questioning their value. Every generation does that. But don't discard the time-tested values upon which civilization is built just because they are old. More important, don't let the doom criers and the cynics persuade you that the best is past — that from here it's all downhill. Each generation goes further than the generation preceding it because it stands on the shoulders of that generation. You will have opportunities beyond anything we've ever known.

— RONALD REAGAN
(speech at University of Notre Dame, 1981)

♦

Opportunities are disguised as hard work, so most people don't recognize them.

— ANN LANDERS

Peace

Lord, thou madest us for thyself,
and we can find no rest
till we find rest in thee.

St. Augustine

To give light to those in darkness and in the shadow of death and to guide our feet into the ways of peace.

— LUKE 1:79

What God Hath Promised

God hath not promised
Skies always blue,
Flower-strewn pathways
All our lives through;
God hath not promised
Sun without rain,
Joy without sorrow,
Peace without pain.

But God hath promised
Strength for the day,
Rest for the labor,
Light for the way,
Grace for the trials,
Help from above,
Unfailing sympathy,
Undying love.

— ANNIE JOHNSON FLINT

The Mystic's Prayer

Lay me to sleep in sheltering flame,
  O Master of the Hidden Fire!
Wash pure my heart, and cleanse for me
  My soul's desire.

In flame of sunrise bathe my mind,
  O Master of the Hidden Fire,
That, when I wake, clear-eyed may be
  My soul's desire.

— FIONA MACLEOD

His Entrance

"Where is the dwelling of God?"
This was the question with which the Rabbi of Kotzk surprised a number of learned men who happened to be visiting him.

They laughed at him. "What a thing to ask! Is not the whole world full of his glory?"

Then he answered his own question. "God dwells wherever man lets him in."

— MARTIN BUBER

Matthew Arnold counted as the greatest single line in all poetry that saying of Dante's poetic insight: "In Thy will is our peace."

— PHILEMON F. STURGES

We spend most of our time and energy in a kind of horizontal thinking. We move along the surface of things going from one quick base to another, often with a frenzy that wears us out. We collect data, things, people, ideas, "profound experiences," never penetrating any of them. . . . But there are other times. There are times when we stop. We sit still. We lose ourselves in a pile of leaves or its memory. We listen and breezes from a whole other world begin to whisper.

— JAMES CARROLL

Pauses

In our whole life melody the music
is broken off here and there by rests,
and we foolishly think we have come
to the end of time. God sends a time
of forced leisure, a time of sickness and
disappointed plans, and makes a sudden
pause in the hymns of our lives, and
we lament that our voice must be silent
and our part missing in the music which
ever goes up to the ear of our Creator.
Not without design does God write the
music of our lives. Be it ours to learn
the time and not be dismayed at the
rests. If we look up, God will beat the
time for us.

— JOHN RUSKIN

◆

Let us not go faster than God. It is our
emptiness and our thirst that he needs,
not our plenitude.

— JACQUES MARITAIN

◆

Prayer

Calm soul of all things! make it mine
To feel, amid the city's jar,
That there abides a peace of thine,
Man did not make, and cannot mar!

The will to neither strive nor cry,
The power to feel with others give!
Calm, calm me more! nor let me die
Before I have begun to live.

— MATTHEW ARNOLD

Secret of Peace

The saints reveal to other men what
a man can be; they smash the body to
atoms and come forth a living flame
with a body newly refreshed; they
unearth the hidden beauty in human
beings who have been passed over as
the waste product of humanity and they
thread together on one golden cord of
the love of God virtues whose existence
was scarcely known, whose combination
seemed incredible, ardor and patience,
meekness and power, detachment and
affection, lowly hope and high humility.
But above all, the saints possess some
secret of peace, as if, like the successful
lover, they were in possession of their
heart's desire, and in this fulfillment
some joy sang within them to which
all their faculties made response. They
are not lonely nor stoical; they are well
acquainted with sorrow and they embrace pain, but everywhere they go they
are accompanied by the sunshine of
spring.

— M. C. D'ARCY

◆

Ultimately, we have just one moral
duty: to reclaim large areas of peace in
ourselves, more and more peace, and
to reflect it toward others. And the
more peace there is in us, the more
peace there will be in our troubled
world.

— ETTY HILLESUM

We, too, the children of the earth, have our moon phases all through any year; the darkness, the delivery from darkness, the waxing and waning. None lives, except the mindless, who does not in some degree experience this; hours of despair followed by hope or, perhaps, slow adjustment; times of fear, even panic, and then the light, however small. For in the normal human being it is impossible to live every day under emotional stress; there have to be, on this seesaw, periods of even balances.

— FAITH BALDWIN

♦

Some people have just enough religion to make them uncomfortable.

— JOHN WESLEY

♦

Fishing

To go fishing is the chance to wash one's soul with pure air, with the rush of the brook, or with the shimmer of the sun on blue water. It brings meekness and inspiration from the decency of nature, charity toward tackle-makers, patience toward fish, a mockery of profits and egos, a quieting of hate, a rejoicing that you do not have to decide a darned thing until next week. And it is discipline in the equality of men — for all men are equal before fish.

— HERBERT HOOVER

I take a sun bath and listen to the hours, formulating, and disintegrating under the pines, and smell the resiny hardi-hood of the high noon hours. The world is lost in a blue haze of distances, and the immediate steeps in a thin and finite sun.

— ZELDA FITZGERALD

♦

All men's miseries derive from not being able to sit quiet in a room alone.

— BLAISE PASCAL

♦

Whatever peace I know rests in the natural world, in feeling myself a part of it, even in a small way.

— MAY SARTON

♦

Have courage for the great sorrows of life and patience for the small ones; and when you have laboriously accomplished your daily task, go to sleep in peace. God is awake.

— VICTOR HUGO

♦

You cannot shake hands with a clenched fist.

— INDIRA GANDHI

Prayer

God warms his hands at
man's heart when he prays.

John Masefield

A prayer in its simplest definition is
merely a wish turned Godward.

— PHILLIPS BROOKS

By all these I pray, by the rolling sun
bursting through untrodden space, a
new ocean of ether every day unveiled.
By the fresh and wandering air encom-
passing the world; by the sea sounding
on the shore — the green sea, white-
flecked at the margin, and the deep
ocean; by the strong earth under me.

— RICHARD JEFFERIES

A *Method of Praying*

1. Be simple and direct in your secret
   prayer. The grace of simplicity is not
   to be despised in public prayer; but
   when we call on God in secret, any
   formality or elaborateness in our
   petitions is an offense.
2. Pray audibly. You need not lift your
   voice to be heard in the street, but it
   is vastly better to pray not merely in
   your thoughts but also with words.
   The utterance of our wants helps to
   define them.
3. Be honest in your secret prayer.
   Do not express any want that you
   do not feel. Do not confess any fault
   that you do not mean to forsake. Do
   not keep anything back. Remember
   that it is He that searcheth the heart
   to whom you are speaking.
4. Pray earnestly. The words need not
   be loud, but the desire should be intense. "The fervent, energetic prayer
   of a righteous man availeth much."
   "The kingdom of heaven suffereth
   violence, and the violent take it by
   force." No listless, drowsy petitioning
   will serve.
5. Do not mock God in your prayers.
   Do not beg him to come to you.
   You know that he is never far from
   any soul that seeks him. That prayer
   is answered before you utter it. Do
   not ask God to do for you that which
   he has expressly bidden you to do.
6. Pray always with special reference
   to the needs of the day and the
   hour; — the warfare to be waged, the
   temptations to be resisted, the work
   to be done, the sorrow to be borne;
   put your life into your prayer; and
   let it be the most real and the most
   immediate business of your life.

— WALTER RAUSCHENBUSCH

And you, who speak in me when I
    speak well,
Withdraw not your grace, leave me
    not dry and cold.
I have praised you in the pain of love,
    I would praise you still
In the slowing of the blood, the time
    when I grow old.

— JUDITH WRIGHT

Prayer is the contemplation of the facts of life from the highest point of view.

— RALPH WALDO EMERSON

◆

Private Prayer

Prayer, the basic exercise of the spirit, must be actively practiced in our private lives. The neglected soul of man must be made strong enough to assert itself once more. For if the power of prayer is again released and used in the lives of common men and women; if the spirit declares its aims clearly and boldly, there is yet hope that our prayers for a better world will be answered.

— ALEXIS CARREL

◆

More things are wrought by prayer
Than this world dreams of.

— ALFRED, LORD TENNYSON

◆

Pray till prayer makes you forget your own wish, and leave it or merge it in God's will.

— FREDERICK W. ROBERTSON

◆

Who riseth from prayer a better man, his prayer is answered.

— GEORGE MEREDITH

Answers

Answers to prayer often come in unexpected ways. We pray, for instance, for a certain virtue; but God seldom delivers Christian virtues all wrapped in a package and ready for use. Rather he puts us in situations where by his help we can develop those virtues. Henry Ward Beecher told of a woman who prayed for patience, and God sent her a poor cook. The best answers to prayer may be the vision and strength to meet a circumstance or to assume a responsibility.

— C. R. FINDLEY

◆

Prayer is not an old woman's idle amusement. Properly understood and applied, it is the most potent instrument of action.

— MAHATMA GANDHI

◆

Lord of the springtime, Father of flower, field and fruit, smile on us in these earnest days when the work is heavy and the toil wearisome; lift up our hearts, O God, to the things worthwhile— sunshine and night, the dripping rain, the song of the birds, books and music, and the voices of our friends. Lift up our hearts to these this night and grant us Thy peace. Amen.

— W. E. B. DU BOIS

Senate Prayers

These prayers by Peter Marshall were given in his capacity of Chaplain of the United States Senate.

I. Our Father, when we long for life without trials and work, without difficulties, remind us that oaks grow strong in contrary winds and diamonds are made under pressure. With stout hearts may we see in every calamity an opportunity and not give way to the pessimist that sees in every opportunity a calamity.

II. Lord, when we are wrong, make us willing to change. And when we are right, make us easy to live with.

III. Let us not be frightened by the problems that confront us, but rather give thee thanks that thou hast matched us with this hour. May we resolve, God helping us, to be part of the answer, and not part of the problem.

IV. Save us from hotheads that would lead us to act foolishly, and from cold feet that would keep us from acting at all. . . .

V. Help us, O Lord, when we want to do the right thing, but know not what it is. But help us most when we know perfectly well what we ought to do, and do not want to do it.

VI. Lord Jesus, thou who art the way, the truth, and the life, hear us as we pray for the truth that shall make men free. Teach us that liberty is not only to be loved but also to be lived. Liberty is too precious a thing to be buried in books. It costs too much to be hoarded. Make us to see that our liberty is not the right to do as we please, but the opportunity to please to do what is right.

VII. Deliver us, we pray thee, from the tyranny of trifles. Teach us how to listen to the prompting of thy Spirit, and thus save us from floundering in indecision that wastes time, subtracts from our peace, divides our efficiency, and multiplies our troubles.

◆

There are times in a man's life when, regardless of the attitude of the body, the soul is on its knees in prayer.

—VICTOR HUGO

◆

Lift up your heart to Him, sometimes even at your meals, and when you are in company; the least little remembrance will always be acceptable to Him. You need not cry very loud; He is nearer to us than we are aware of.

—BROTHER LAWRENCE

Testimony

Personal prayer, it seems to me, is one of the simplest necessities of life, as basic to the individual as sunshine, food and water—and at times, of course, more so. By prayer I believe we mean an effort to get in touch with the Infinite. We know that our prayers are imperfect. Of course they are. We are imperfect human beings. A thousand experiences have convinced me beyond room of doubt that prayer multiplies the strength of the individual and brings within the scope of his capabilities almost any conceivable objective.

— DWIGHT D. EISENHOWER

♦

Absolute unmixed attention is prayer.

— SIMONE WEIL

♦

Two-Way Street

Prayer is neither black magic nor is it a form of demand note. Prayer is a relationship. The act of praying is more analogous to clearing away the underbrush which shuts out a view than it is to begging in the street. There are many different kinds of prayer. Yet all prayer has one basic purpose. We pray not to get something, but to open up a two-way street between us and God, so that we and others may inwardly become something.

— JOHN HEUSS

The privilege of prayer to me is one of the most cherished possessions, because faith and experience alike convince me that God himself sees and answers, and his answers I never venture to criticize. It is only my part to ask. If it were otherwise, I would not dare to pray at all.

— WILFRED T. GRENFELL

♦

O god, thy sea is so great,
and my boat is so small.

— PRAYER OF
BRETON FISHERMEN

♦

Prayer is not the moment when God and humans are in relationship, for that is always. Prayer is taking initiative to intentionally respond to God's presence.

— L. ROBERT KECK

♦

The Unseen Bridge

There is a bridge whereof the span
Is hidden in the heart of man,
And reaches, without pile or rod,
Into the plenitude of God.

It carries all that honestly
Is faith or hope or charity.
No other traffic will it bear:
This broad yet narrow Bridge
    of Prayer.

— GILBERT THOMAS

Prayer

Nine Memorable Prayers

I.

O God, grant us the serenity to accept what
cannot be changed; the courage to change
what should be changed; and wisdom to dis-
tinguish one from the other.

— REINHOLD NIEBUHR

II.

Beloved Pan, and all ye other gods who haunt this place,
give me beauty in the inward soul; and may the outward
and inward man be at one.

— SOCRATES

III.

Grant us grace, Almighty Father, so
to pray as to deserve to be heard.

— JANE AUSTEN

IV.

Great Spirit, help me never to judge another
until I have walked in his moccasins.

— SIOUX INDIAN

V.

O Lord, thou knowest that which is best for us. Let this or that
be done, as thou shalt please. Give what thou wilt, how much
thou wilt, and when thou wilt.

— THOMAS À KEMPIS

VI.

O Lord, thou knowest how busy I must be this day.
If I forget thee, do not thou forget me.

— LORD ASHLEY

VII.

May the wisdom of God instruct me, the eye of God
watch over me, the ear of God hear me, the word of
God give me sweet talk, the hand of God defend me,
the way of God guide me.
Christ be with me.
Christ before me.
Christ in me.
Christ under me.
Christ over me.
Christ on my right hand.
Christ on my left hand.
Christ on this side.
Christ on that side.
Christ in the head of everyone to whom I speak.
Christ in the mouth of every person who speaks to me.
Christ in the eye of every person who looks upon me.
Christ in the ear of everyone who hears me today.
  Amen.

—ST. PATRICK

VIII.

Father in Heaven, when the thought of thee wakes
in our hearts, let it not awaken like a frightened
bird that flies about in dismay, but like a child
waking from its sleep with a heavenly smile.

—SØREN KIERKEGAARD

IX.

Teach us, good Lord, to serve thee as thou deservest:
    to give and not to count the cost;
    to fight and not to heed the wounds;
    to toil and not to seek for rest;
    to labor and not to ask for any reward
    save that of knowing that we do thy will.

—ST. IGNATIUS OF LOYOLA

He that enjoys aught without thanksgiving is as though he robbed God.

— ST. JOHN CHRYSOSTOM

♦

A *Meditation on the Lord's Prayer*
Our Father, who art in heaven.
Help me to believe this day that
there is a power to lift me up which
is stronger than all the things that
hold me down.

Hallowed be Thy Name.
Help me to be sensitive to what is
beautiful, and responsive to what is
good, so that day by day I may grow
more sure of the holiness of life in
which I want to trust.

Thy Kingdom come.
Help me to be quick to see, and
ready to encourage, whatever brings
the better meaning of God into that
which otherwise might be the common round of the uninspired day.

Thy will be done, on earth as it is
in heaven.
Help me to believe that the ideals of
the spirit are not a far-off dream, but
a power to command loyalty and
direct my life here on our real earth.

Give us this day our daily bread.
Open the way for me to earn an
honest living without anxiety; but
let me never forget the needs of
others, and make me want only

that benefit for myself which will
also be their gain.

And forgive us our trespasses, as we forgive
those who trespass against us.
Make me patient and sympathetic
with the shortcomings of others,
especially of those I love; and keep
me sternly watchful only of my own.
Let me never grow hard with the
unconscious cruelty of those who
measure themselves by mean standards, and so think they have
excelled. Keep my eyes lifted to the
highest, so that I may be forgiving,
because I know how much there is
of which I need to be forgiven.

And lead us not into temptation, but
deliver us from evil.
Let me not go carelessly this day
within the reach of any evil I cannot
resist, but if in the path of duty I
must go where temptation is, give
me strength of spirit to meet it
without fear.

For thine is the kingdom, and the power,
and the glory for ever and ever. Amen.

— WALTER RUSSELL BOWIE

♦

Step softly, under snow or rain,
To find the place where men can pray;
The way is all so very plain
That we may lose the way.

— GILBERT KEITH CHESTERTON

Principle

Faithfully faithful to every trust,
Honestly honest in every deed,
Righteously righteous and justly just:
This is the whole of the good man's creed.

Resolution

Let then our first act every morning be
    to make the following resolve for
    the day:
I shall not fear anyone on earth.
I shall fear only God.
I shall not bear ill will toward anyone.
I shall not submit to injustice from
    anyone.
I shall conquer untruth by truth.
And in resisting untruth I shall put up
    with all suffering.

— MAHATMA GANDHI

♦

Ten Spiritual Tonics

1. *Stop worrying.* Worry kills life.
2. *Begin each day with a prayer.* It will
    arm your soul.
3. *Control appetite.* Over-indulgence
    clogs body and mind.
4. *Accept your limitations.* All of us can't
    be great.
5. *Don't envy.* It wastes time and energy.
6. *Have faith in people.* Cynicism sours
    the disposition.
7. *Find a hobby.* It will relax your
    nerves.
8. *Read a book a week* to stimulate
    imagination and broaden your view.
9. *Spend some time alone,* for the peace
    of solitude and silence.
10. *Try to want what you have,* instead of
    spending your strength trying to get
    what you want.

— ABRAHAM L. FEINBERG

But warm, eager, living life — to be
rooted in life — to learn, to desire to
know, to feel, to think, to act. That is
what I want. And nothing less. That
is what I must try for.

— KATHERINE MANSFIELD

♦

My Purpose

To awaken each morning with a smile
    brightening my face;
To greet the day with reverence for the
    opportunities it contains;
To approach my work with a clean
    mind;
To hold ever before me, even in the
    doing of little things, the Ultimate
    Purpose toward which I am
    working;
To meet men and women with laughter
    on my lips and love in my heart;
To be gentle, kind, and courteous
    through all the hours;
To approach the night with weariness
    that ever woos sleep, and the joy that
    comes from work well done —
This is how I desire to waste wisely my
    days.

— THOMAS DEKKER

♦

Most people are willing to take the
Sermon on the Mount as a flag to sail
under, but few will use it as a rudder
by which to steer.

— OLIVER WENDELL HOLMES

I cannot and will not cut my conscience
to fit this year's fashions.

> —LILLIAN HELLMAN

◆

Windows of the Soul

Let there be many windows in your
   soul,
That all the glory of the universe
May beautify it. Not the narrow pane
Of one poor creed can catch the
   radiant rays
That shine from countless sources.
   Tear away
The blinds of superstition. Let the light
Pour through fair windows, broad as
   truth itself,
And high as heaven . . . Tune your ear
To all the wordless music of the stars,
And to the voice of Nature; and your
   heart
Shall turn to truth and goodness as
   the plant
Turns to the sun. A thousand unseen
   hands
Reach down to help you to their peace-
   crowned heights;
And all the forces of the firmament
Shall fortify your strength. Be not afraid
To thrust aside half-truths and grasp the
   whole.

> —ELLA WHEELER WILCOX

◆

Never lose a holy curiosity.

> —ALBERT EINSTEIN

My son, resolve to do the will of others
   rather than your own.
Always choose to possess less rather than
   more.
Always take the lowest place, and regard
   yourself as less than others.
Desire and pray always that God's will
   may be perfectly fulfilled in you.
A man who observes these rules shall
   enjoy peace and tranquility of soul.

> —THOMAS À KEMPIS

◆

Always fall in with what you're asked to
accept. Take what is given, and make it
your own way. My aim in life has always
been to hold my own with whatever's
going. Not against: with.

> —ROBERT FROST

◆

When you know what your values are,
making decisions becomes easier.

> —GLENN VAN ECKEREN

◆

My creed is this:
   Justice is the only worship;
   Love is the only priest;
   Ignorance is the only slavery;
   Happiness is the only good;
   The time to be happy is now,
   The place to be happy is here,
   The way to be happy is to
      make others so.

> —ROBERT INGERSOLL

My Task

To be honest, to be kind;
To earn a little and to spend a little less;
To make upon the whole a family hap-
pier for his presence;
To renounce when that shall be neces-
sary and not to be embittered;
To keep a few friends, but those without
capitulation;
Above all, on the same grim conditions,
to keep friends with himself—
Here is a task for all that man has of
fortitude and delicacy.

— ROBERT LOUIS STEVENSON

♦

Give the best you have received from
the past to the best that you may come
to know in the future.

Accept life daily not as a cup to be
drained but as a chalice to be filled
with whatsoever things are honest, pure,
lovely, and of good report. Making a
living is best undertaken as a part of the
more important business of making
a life.

Every now and again take a good look
at something not made with hands—
a mountain, a star, the turn of a stream.
There will come to you wisdom and
patience and solace and, above all, the
assurance that you are not alone in the
world.

— SIDNEY LOVETT

Thomas Jefferson's Decalogue

I. Never put off till tomorrow what you can do today.

II. Never trouble another for what you can do yourself.

III. Never spend your money before you have it.

IV. Never buy what you do not want, because it is cheap; it will be dear to you.

V. Pride costs us more than hunger, thirst, and cold.

VI. We never repent of having eaten too little.

VII. Nothing is troublesome that we do willingly.

VIII. How much pain have cost us the evils which have never happened.

IX. Take things always by their smooth handle.

X. When angry, count ten, before you speak; if very angry, an hundred.

♦

My creed is that public service must
be more than doing a job efficiently and
honestly. It must be a complete dedica-
tion to the people and to the nation
with full recognition that every human
being is entitled to courtesy and consideration, that constructive criticism is
not only to be expected but sought, that
smears are not only to be expected but
fought, that honor is to be earned not
bought.

— MARGARET CHASE SMITH

I believe in one God, and no more;
and I hope for happiness beyond this
life. I believe in the equality of man; and
I believe that religious duties consist in
doing justice, loving mercy, and endeav-
oring to make our fellow creatures
happy.

— THOMAS PAINE

♦

Our life is frittered away by detail. . . .
I say, let your affairs be as two or three,
and not a hundred or a thousand; instead of a million count half a dozen,
and keep your accounts on your thumb-
nail. . . . Simplify, simplify. Instead
of three meals a day, if it be necessary
eat but one; instead of a hundred
dishes, five; and reduce other things
in proportion.

Let us spend every day as deliberately
as Nature, and not be thrown off the
track by every nutshell and mosquito's
wing that falls on the rails.

— HENRY DAVID THOREAU

♦

Be kind; everyone you meet is fighting a
hard battle.

— JOHN WATSON

♦

Let us, then, be what we are; speak
what we think; and in all things keep
ourselves loyal to truth.

— HENRY WADSWORTH
LONGFELLOW

Abraham Lincoln's Creed
I believe in God, the Almighty Ruler of
nations, our great and good and merci-
ful Maker, our Father in heaven, who
notes the fall of a sparrow and numbers
the hairs on our heads. I recognize the
sublime truth announced in the Holy
Scriptures and proved by all history that
those nations are blessed whose God is
the Lord. I believe that the will of God
prevails. Without him, all human reli-
ance is vain. With that assistance I
cannot fail. I have a solemn vow regis-
tered in heaven to finish the work I am
in, in full view of my responsibility to
my God, with malice toward none; with
charity for all; with firmness in the right,
as God gives me to see the right.

— COMPILED BY
WILLIAM E. BARTON

♦

Learn from the earliest days to insure
your principles against the perils of ridicule. If you think it right to differ from
the times, and to make a stand for any
valuable point of morals, do it, however
rustic, however antiquated, however
pedantic it may appear; do it, not for
insolence, but seriously, and grandly, as
a man who wears a soul of his own in
his bosom, and does not wait till it shall
be breathed into him by the breath of
fashion.

— SYDNEY SMITH

I Believe

I believe in the supreme worth of the individual and in his right to life, liberty, and the pursuit of happiness.

I believe that every right implies a responsibility; every opportunity, an obligation; every possession, a duty.

I believe that the law was made for man and not man for the law; that government is the servant of the people and not their master.

I believe in the dignity of labor, whether with head or hand; that the world owes no man a living but that it owes every man an opportunity to make a living.

I believe that thrift is essential to well-ordered living and that economy is a prime requisite of a sound financial structure, whether in government, business, or personal affairs.

I believe that truth and justice are fundamental to an enduring social order.

I believe in the sacredness of a promise, that a man's word should be as good as his bond; that character — not wealth or power or position — is of supreme worth.

I believe that the rendering of useful service is the common duty of mankind and that only in the purifying fire of sacrifice is the dross of selfishness consumed and the greatness of the human soul set free.

I believe in an all-wise and all-loving God, named by whatever name, and that the individual's highest fulfillment, greatest happiness, and widest usefulness are to be found in living in harmony with His will.

I believe that love is the greatest thing in the world; that it alone can overcome hate; that right can and will triumph over might.

—JOHN D. ROCKEFELLER, JR.

Religion

The universe is centered on
neither the earth nor the sun.
It is centered on God.

Alfred Noyes

The only struggle which religions can justify, the only struggle worthy of man, is the moral struggle against man's own disordered passions against every kind of selfishness, against attempts to oppress others, against every type of hatred and violence.

— POPE JOHN PAUL II

Religion does not occupy any one part of man's life. It is the reaction of a man's whole being to his object of highest loyalty. Religion must be felt and thought. It must be lived out; it must translate itself into action. Religion is not a segment of life, nor is it connected with any one time or place. It is not just ritual, ceremony, doctrines, or the church, even though these may all be aids in stimulating it. The great religious leaders of the race have spoken of religion as a vital, personal experience. This experience grows out of real needs — the need for courage and companionship in life. Micah speaks of man's chief duty "To love mercy, to do justly, and to walk humbly with thy God." For Jesus the great commandments were love of God and love of one's neighbor. Whether religion has been interpreted as man's cooperative quest for the values of life or as "the Spirit of God in the soul of man," it has been stressed as involving the whole of life.

— HAROLD H. TITUS

Shall I say: Creator, Sustainer, Pardoner, Near One, Distant One, Incomprehensible One, God both of flowers and stars, God of the gentle wind and of terrible battles, Wisdom, Power, Loyalty and Truthfulness, Eternity and Infinity, you the All-Merciful, you the Just One, you Love itself?

— KARL RAHNER

The Goal
All roads that lead to God are good;
What matters it, your faith or mine;
Both center at the goal divine
Of love's eternal brotherhood.

A thousand creeds have come and gone;
But what is that to you or me?
Creeds are but branches of a tree,
The root of love lives on and on.

Though branch by branch proves
     withered wood,
The root is warm with precious wine;
Then keep your faith, and leave me
     mine;
All roads that lead to God are good.

— ELLA WHEELER WILCOX

God is not finished. His highest divine attribute is His creativeness and that which is creative exists always in the beginning stage. God is eternally in Genesis.

— ISAAC BASHEVIS SINGER

It is only by forgetting yourself that you draw near to God.

— HENRY DAVID THOREAU

♦

Experiment

In its essence the Gospel is a call to make the experiment of comradeship, the experiment of fellowship, the experiment of trusting the heart of things, throwing self-care to the winds, in the sure and certain faith that you will not be deserted, forsaken nor betrayed, and that your ultimate interests are perfectly secure in the hands of the Great Companion. This insight is the center, the kernel, the growing point of the Christian religion, which, when we have it, all else is secure, and when we have it not, all else is precarious.

— L. P. JACKS

♦

The nature of God is a circle whose center is everywhere and whose circumference is nowhere.

— ST. AUGUSTINE

♦

Science and religion, religion and science, put it as I may, they are two sides of the same glass, through which we see darkly until these two, focusing together, reveal the truth.

— PEARL BUCK

The wonderful thing about saints is that they were *human*. They lost their tempers, got hungry, scolded God, were egotistical or testy or impatient in their turns, made mistakes and regretted them. Still they went on doggedly blundering toward heaven.

— PHYLLIS MC GINLEY

♦

What is your religion? I mean — not what you know about religion but the belief that helps you most?

— GEORGE ELIOT

♦

What Is God?

Creator of minds to receive his own
    fullness,
imparting to them life to be conscious
    of him,
prompting them to desire him,
enlarging them to receive him,
fitting them to be worthy of him,
enkindling them with zeal,
aiding them to yield fruit,
directing them to equity,
fashioning them to benevolence,
tempering them for wisdom,
strengthening them for virtue,
visiting them for consolation,
illuminating them for knowledge,
preserving them for immortality,
enriching them for felicity,
surrounding them with protection.

— ST. BERNARD OF CLAIRVAUX

What Is Religion?

Religion in the life of man is a momentary glance from time into eternity.

It is Augustine visioning his *Civitas Dei* when the City of Man is about
to crumble.

It is Pythagoras discerning eternal truths in the framework of a right triangle.

It is Plato grasping Beauty, Truth, and Goodness as eternal verities through
human reason.

It is Edna St. Vincent Millay writing "Renascence" and crying out,

> The soul can split the sky in two,
> And let the fact of God shine through

It is Socrates saying, "Knowledge is virtue."

It is Newton at twenty-four discovering the binomial theorem and the law
of gravitation.

It is Handel with a paralyzed limb, destitute of money, facing imprisonment,
gathering new courage and writing his greatest oratorio, *The Messiah.*

It is Paul hearing the voice of his Lord on the Damascus Road.

It is Jesus in terrible agony crying, "Father, into thy hands I commit my
spirit."

It is an ordinary man dedicating every fiber of himself to the betterment
of the world.

It is Albrecht Dürer painting his "Praying Hands."

It is Washington praying alone at Valley Forge.

It is Isaiah changing his purple garments of a prince for the tattered cloth
of a prophet to save a nation from chaos.

It is Augustine forsaking a lustful heart and fleeing into the arms of God, and
later becoming the Bishop of Hippo.

It is a priest jotting down the last words of a dying marine at Guadalcanal and
composing a letter of comfort to a widowed mother in St. Louis.

It is Jesus saying to his disciples, "Take up your cross and follow me."

It is a teacher refusing a gainful salary elsewhere that he may instruct youth
in the wisdom of the ages.

It is Mary weeping at the foot of the cross.

It is Clement of Alexandria interpreting the divine Logos as the inspiration
for all truth.

It is a father sacrificing a suit of clothes that his son may stay in college.

It is a widow in a tenement taking in washing to support three orphaned children of a former neighbor across the hall.

It is Luther standing firm at Worms saying, "I cannot and will not recant anything, since it is unsafe and dangerous to do anything against the conscience."

It is Francis of Assisi preaching to the birds and the flowers.

It is a man centering his focus on God and not himself, and finding his life changed from a state of worry to a state of wonder.

It is Edith Cavell before a firing squad in Brussels saying, "Patriotism is not enough."

It is a man saying, "My soul is so absorbed in the bigger issues of life that I cannot afford to be jealous and suspicious of any person."

It is the sacrifice of a meal by an American family in order that starvation elsewhere may be averted.

It is Bernard at a monastery in Clairvaux in love with Christ and married to the church.

It is Servetus burning at the stake in Geneva for the sake of truth.

It is Amos forsaking his flock at Tekoa to preach against hypocrisy at Bethel.

It is Schleiermacher discerning religion as man's feeling of absolute dependence upon God.

It is Katherine Mansfield saying about her literary creations shortly before her death, "Not one of these writings dare I show to God."

It is Thomas Aquinas wedding reason and faith.

It is my feeling of humility when I contemplate God as the Life of a universe extending a million light years into space.

It is Deutero-Isaiah discerning the nations as specks of sand when compared to God's majesty and infinity.

It is my little self on a second-rate planet eradicating fear, self-centeredness, resentment, and guilt in order that it may become an instrument of God's energetic redemptive love.

It is the writer of the Gospel of John reporting, "Let not your hearts be troubled; believe in God."

Yes, these are all religion. For religion is as big as life and as normal an experience as breathing, eating, and sleeping.

—THOMAS S. KEPLER

God's Medicine

During the past thirty years, people from all civilized countries on the earth have consulted me. Among all my patients in the second half of life—that is to say, over thirty-five—there has not been one whose problem in the last resort was not that of finding a religious outlook on life. It is safe to say that every one of them fell ill because he had lost that which the living religions of every age have given to their followers, and none of them has been really healed who did not regain his religious outlook.

—C. G. JUNG

♦

Jesus is God spelling himself out in language that man can understand.

—S. D. GORDON

♦

God Be in My Head

God be in my head,
  And in my understanding;

God be in my eyes,
  And in my looking;

God be in my mouth,
  And in my speaking;

God be in my heart,
  And in my thinking;

God be at my end,
  And at my departing.

—SARUM PRIMER

Religion should be our steering wheel, not our spare tire.

—CHARLES L. WHEELER

♦

I believe in God as I believe in my friends, because I feel the breathe of His affections, feel His invisible hand, drawing me, leading me, grasping me; because I possess an inner consciousness of a particular Providence and of a universal mind that marks out for me the course of my own destiny.

—MIGUEL DE UNAMUNO

♦

There's a divinity that shapes our ends,
  Rough hew them how we will.

—WILLIAM SHAKESPEARE

♦

The church must be reminded that it is not the master or the servant of the state, but rather the conscience of the state.

—MARTIN LUTHER KING, JR.

♦

All outward forms of religion are almost useless, and are the causes of endless strife. . . . Believe there is a great power silently working all things for good, behave yourself and never mind the rest.

—BEATRIX POTTER

The essential thing to know about God is that God is Good. All the rest is secondary.

— SIMONE WEIL

The heart of the Christian Gospel is precisely that God is the all holy One; the all powerful One is also the One full of mercy and compassion. He is not a neutral God inhabiting some inaccessible Mount Olympus. He is a God who cares about his children and cares enormously for the weak, the poor, the naked, the downtrodden, the despised. He takes their side not because they are good, since many of them are demonstrably not so. He takes their side because He is that kind of God, and they have no one else to champion them.

— DESMOND TUTU

If you think about it, you will find that there is no meaning of life if you are estranged from God.

— CATHERINE BRAMWELL-BOOTH

No man has a right to lead such a life of contemplation as to forget in his own ease the service due to his neighbor; nor has any man a right to be so immersed in active life as to neglect the contemplation of God.

— ST. AUGUSTINE

We have been looking for the burning bush, the parting of the sea, the bellowing voice from heaven. Instead we should be looking at the ordinary day-by-day events in our lives for evidence of the miraculous.

— M. SCOTT PECK

He who knows about depths knows about God.

— PAUL TILLICH

This is what I found out about religion: it gives you courage to make the decisions you must make in a crisis and the confidence to leave the results to a higher Power. Only by trust in God can a man carrying responsibility find repose.

— DWIGHT D. EISENHOWER

Religion means faith that man's ideals are achievable and will be achieved.

— JEROME FRANK

There is no religion without love, and people may talk as much as they like about their religion, but if it does not teach them to be good and kind to man and beast, it is all a sham.

— ANNA SEWELL

Certainty

Religion exists not to answer all questions, or to clear up all mysteries; if that were its purpose, it could never be accomplished, for life
grows, not less, but more mysterious as the intellect enters more fully
into its truth.

The stars were wonderful enough in all conscience, when we
thought of them as lamps of light set in a solid sky to guide the
sailors on their journey over the trackless sea; but they are a million
times more wonderful, now that we know them to be blazing worlds,
that move through the vast infinities of space in accordance with
exact mathematical laws.

Our own bodies were wonderful enough, when we thought of
them as created in a moment by the fiat of the Almighty from the
dust of the earth; but how much more wonderful they have become
since the sciences of physiology and embryology have taught us to
trace their growth through countless stages, from the humblest kind
of beginning to their present complex end.

Knowledge does not take from, it adds to, the wonder of the
world. It is an infallible rule that the more a man knows the less he
knows. He knows that he knows nothing compared with what there
is to know—that he is but a child playing on the shore of an infinite
sea of truth and picking up tiny pearls of wisdom that, by the grace
of God, are cast up at his feet.

Religion leaves a million questions unanswered and apparently
unanswerable. Its purpose and object is not to make a man certain
and cock-sure about everything, but to make him certain about those
things of which he must be certain if he is to live a human life at all.
Religion does not relieve us from the duty of thought; it makes
possible for a man to begin thinking.

—G. A. STUDDERT-KENNEDY

Thankfulness

A single grateful thought toward heaven
is the most complete prayer.

Gotthold Lessing

Prayer

Oh, Lord, I thank you for the privilege and gift of living in a world filled with beauty and excitement and variety.

I thank you for the gift of loving and being loved, for the friendliness and understanding and beauty of the animals on the farm and in the forest and marshes, for the green of the trees, the sound of a waterfall, the darting beauty of the trout in the brook.

I thank you for the delights of music and children, of other men's thoughts and conversation and their books to read by the fireside or in bed with the rain falling on the roof or the snow blowing past outside the window.

— LOUIS BROMFIELD

♦

Gratitude is the heart's memory.

— FRENCH PROVERB

♦

Praise him with the sound of the
    trumpet: praise him with psaltery
    and harp.
Praise him with the timbrel and dance:
    praise him with stringed instruments
    and organs.
Praise him upon the loud cymbals:
    praise him upon the high sounding
    cymbals.
Let every thing that hath breath praise
    the Lord.

— PSALM 150:3–6

In ordinary life we hardly realize that we receive a great deal more than we give, and that it is only with gratitude that life becomes rich. It is very easy to overestimate the importance of our own achievements in comparison with what we owe others.

— DIETRICH BONHOEFFER

♦

My poems are hymns of praise to the glory of life.

— EDITH SITWELL

♦

Thank You

It was inevitable, I suppose, that in the garden I should begin, at long last, to ask myself what lay behind all this beauty. When guests were gone and I had the flowers to myself, I was so happy that I wondered why at the same time I was haunted by a sense of emptiness. It was as though I wanted to thank somebody, but had nobody to thank; which is another way of saying that I felt the need for worship. That is, perhaps, the kindliest way in which a man may come to his God. There is an interminable literature on the origins of the religious impulse, but to me it is simpler than that. It is summed up in the image of a man at sundown, watching the crimson flowering of the sky and saying — to somebody — "Thank you."

— BEVERLY NICHOLS

Gratitude consists in a watchful, minute attention to the particulars of our state, and to the multitude of God's gifts, taken one by one. It fills us with a consciousness that God loves and cares for us, even to the least event and smallest need of life. It is a blessed thought that from our childhood God has been laying his fatherly hands upon us, and always in benediction, and that even the strokes of his hands are blessings, and among the chiefest we have ever received.

— HENRY EDWARD MANNING

◆

Gratitude is not only the greatest of virtues, but the parent of all the others.

— CICERO

◆

To those of us who study history not merely as a reminder of man's follies and crimes, but also as an encouraging remembrance of generative souls, the past ceases to be a depressing chamber of horrors; it becomes a celestial city, a spacious country of the mind, wherein a thousand saints, statesmen, inventors, scientists, poets, artists, musicians, lovers, and philosophers still live and speak, teach and carve and sing.

— WILL DURANT

Some people always sigh in thanking God.

— ELIZABETH BARRETT BROWNING

◆

The bridegroom may forget the bride,
  Was made his wedded wife yestreen;
The monarch may forget the crown
  That on his head an hour has been;
The mother may forget the child
  That smiles sae sweetly on her knee;
But I'll remember thee, Glencairn,
  And a' that thou hast done for me.

— ROBERT BURNS

◆

To stand on one leg and prove God's existence is a very different thing from going down on one's knees and thanking him.

— SØREN KIERKEGAARD

◆

It was easier to do a friendly thing than it was to stay and be thanked for it.

— LOUISA MAY ALCOTT

◆

A man's indebtedness . . . is not virtue; his repayment is. Virtue begins when he dedicates himself actively to the job of gratitude.

— RUTH BENEDICT

The Art of Thanksgiving

The art of thanksgiving is thanksliving. It is gratitude in action. It is applying Albert Schweitzer's philosophy: "In gratitude for your own good fortune you must render in return some sacrifice of your life for other life."

It is thanking God for the gift of life by living it triumphantly.

It is thanking God for your talents and abilities by accepting them as obligations to be invested for the common good.

It is thanking God for all that men and women have done for you by doing things for others.

It is thanking God for opportunities by accepting them as a challenge to achievement.

It is thanking God for happiness by striving to make others happy.

It is thanking God for beauty by helping to make the world more beautiful.

It is thanking God for inspiration by trying to be an inspiration to others.

It is thanking God for health and strength by the care and reverence you show your body.

It is thanking God for the creative ideas that enrich life by adding your own creative contributions to human progress.

It is thanking God for each new day by living it to the fullest.

It is thanking God by giving hands, arms, legs, and voice to your thankful spirit.

It is adding to your prayers of thanksgiving, acts of thanksliving.

—WILFERD A. PETERSON

Today

I have no Yesterdays,
Time took them away;
Tomorrow may not be—
But I have Today.

Pearl Yeadon McGinnis

Procrastination

One of the most tragic things I know about human nature is that all of us tend to put off living. We are all dreaming of some magical rose garden over the horizon—instead of enjoying the roses that are blooming outside our windows today.

— DALE CARNEGIE

♦

The Salutation of the Dawn

Listen to the Exhortation of the Dawn!
Look to this Day!
For it is Life, the very Life of Life.
In its brief course lie all the
Verities and Realities of your Existence:
  The Bliss of Growth,
  The Glory of Action,
  The Splendor of Beauty,
For Yesterday is but a Dream,
And Tomorrow is only a Vision:
But Today well-lived makes
Every Yesterday a Dream of Happiness,
And every Tomorrow a Vision of Hope.
Look well therefore to this Day!
Such is the Salutation of the Dawn!

— BASED ON THE SANSKRIT

♦

My candle burns at both its ends;
  It will not last the night;
But oh, my foes, and oh, my friends—
  It gives a lovely light.

— EDNA ST. VINCENT MILLAY

Today

So here hath been dawning
  Another blue day:
Think, wilt thou let it
  Slip useless away?

Out of Eternity
  This new day is born;
Into Eternity,
  At night, will return

Behold it aforetime
  No eye ever did;
So soon it forever
  From all eyes is hid.

Here hath been dawning
  Another blue day:
Think, wilt thou let it
  Slip useless away?

— THOMAS CARLYLE

♦

One Day at a Time

Finish every day and be done with it. You have done what you could. Some blunders and absurdities no doubt crept in; forget them as soon as you can. Tomorrow is a new day; begin it well and serenely and with too high a spirit to be cumbered with your old nonsense. This day is all that is good and fair. It is too dear, with its hopes and invitations, to waste a moment on yesterdays.

— RALPH WALDO EMERSON

Today is the only time we can possibly live.

— DALE CARNEGIE

◆

To every thing there is a season, and a
   time to every purpose under heaven;
A time to be born, and a time to die; a
   time to plant, and a time to pluck
   up that which is planted;
A time to kill, and a time to heal; a
   time to break down and a time to
   build up;
A time to weep, and a time to laugh; a
   time to mourn, and a time to dance;
A time to cast away stones, and a time
   to gather stones together; a time
   to embrace, and a time to refrain
   from embracing;
A time to get, and a time to lose; a time
   to keep, and a time to cast away;
A time to rend, and a time to sew; a
   time to keep silence, and a time
   to speak;
A time to love, and a time to hate; a
   time of war, and a time of peace.

— ECCLESIASTES 3:1–8

◆

There is a kind of release that comes
directly to those who have undergone
an ordeal and who know, having sur-
vived it, that they are equal to all of
life's occasions.

— LEWIS MUMFORD

He who every morning plans the trans-
actions of the day and follows out that
plan carries a thread that will guide him
through the labyrinth of the most busy
life. The orderly arrangement of his time
is like a ray of light which darts itself
through all his occupations. But where
no plan is laid, where the disposal of
time is surrendered merely to the chance
of incidents, chaos will soon reign.

— VICTOR HUGO

◆

If you let yourself be absorbed completely, if you surrender completely
to the moments as they pass, you live
more richly those moments.

— ANNE MORROW LINDBERGH

◆

We live on a moving line between past
and future. That line is our lifeline.

— GEORGE A. BUTTRICK

◆

I expect to pass through the world but
once. Any good therefore that I can do,
or any kindness or abilities that I can
show to any fellow creature, let me do it
now. Let me not defer or neglect it, for
I shall not pass this way again.

— WILLIAM PENN

Today

Just for Today

Just for today, I will try to live through this day only, and not tackle my whole life problem at once. I can do something for twelve hours that would appall me if I felt that I had to keep it up for a lifetime.

Just for today, I will be happy. This assumes to be true what Abraham Lincoln said, that "most folks are as happy as they make up their minds to be."

Just for today, I will try to strengthen my mind. I will study. I will learn something useful. I will not be a mental loafer. I will read something that requires effort, thought and concentration.

Just for today, I will adjust myself to what is, and not try to adjust everything to my own desires. I will take my "luck" as it comes, and fit myself to it.

Just for today, I will exercise my soul in three ways: I will do somebody a good turn, and not get found out. I will do at least two things I don't want to do — just for exercise. I will not show anyone that my feelings are hurt; they may be hurt, but today I will not show it.

Just for today, I will be agreeable. I will look as well as I can, dress becomingly, talk low, act courteously, criticize not one bit, not find fault with anything and not try to improve or regulate anybody except myself.

Just for today, I will have a program. I may not follow it exactly, but I will have it. I will save myself from two pests: hurry and indecision.

Just for today, I will have a quiet half hour all by myself, and relax. During this half hour, sometime, I will try to get a better perspective of my life.

Just for today, I will be unafraid. Especially I will not be afraid to enjoy what is beautiful, and to believe that as I give to the world, so the world will give to me.

— KENNETH L. HOLMES

Wisdom

The journey of a thousand miles
begins with one step.

Lao-tzu

A mature person is one who does not think only in absolutes, who is able to be objective even when deeply stirred emotionally, who has learned that there is both good and bad in all people and in all things, and who walks humbly and deals charitably with the circumstances of life, knowing that in this world no one is all knowing and therefore all of us need both love and charity.

— ELEANOR ROOSEVELT

♦

The best cosmetic in the world is an active mind that is always finding something new.

— MARY MEEK ATKESON

♦

The human face is really like one of those Oriental gods: a whole group of faces juxtaposed on different planes; it is impossible to see them all simultaneously.

— MARCEL PROUST

♦

To mature is in part to realize that while complete intimacy and omniscience and power cannot be had, self-transcendence, growth, and closeness to others are nevertheless within one's reach.

— SISSELA BOX

Lessons History Teaches
When it gets dark enough,
you can see the stars.
The bee fertilizes the flower that it robs.
Whom the gods would destroy,
they first make mad.
The mills of the gods grind slowly,
but they grind exceeding fine.

— CHARLES A. BEARD

♦

When speculation has done its worst, two and two still make four.

— SAMUEL JOHNSON

♦

Wisdom About Life
The differences in human life depend, for the most part, not on what men do, but upon the meaning and purpose of their acts. All are born, all die, all lose their loved ones, nearly all marry and nearly all work, but the significance of these acts may vary enormously. The same physical act may be in one situation vulgar and in another holy. The same work may be elevating or degrading. The major question is not "What act do I perform?" but "In what frame do I put it?" Wisdom about life consists in taking the inevitable ventures which are the very stuff of common existence, and glorifying them.

— ELTON TRUEBLOOD

There are years that ask questions and years that answer.

— ZORA NEALE HURSTON

•

To be a philosopher is not merely to have subtle thoughts, nor even to found a school, but so to love wisdom as to live, according to its dictates, a life of simplicity, independence, magnanimity, and trust.

— HENRY DAVID THOREAU

•

Besides the noble art of getting things done, there is the noble art of leaving things undone. The wisdom of life consists in the elimination of nonessentials.

— LIN YUTANG

•

The Heart's Reasons
The heart has its reasons, which reason does not know. We feel it in a thousand things. I say that the heart naturally loves the Universal Being, and also itself naturally, according as it gives itself to them; and it hardens itself against one or the other at its will.

— BLAISE PASCAL

•

All discoveries in art and science result from an accumulation of errors.

— MARSHALL MC LUHAN

Whoever it was who searched the heavens with a telescope and found no God would not have found the human mind if he had searched the brain with a microscope.

— GEORGE SANTAYANA

•

Adventure of Faith
My message has been very simple. To live well we must have a faith fit to live by, a self fit to live with, and a work fit to live for — something to which we can give ourselves and thus get ourselves off our hands. We cannot tell what may happen to us in the strange medley of life. But we can decide what happens in us — how we can take it, what we do with it — and that is what really counts in the end. How to take the raw stuff of life and make it a thing of worth and beauty — that is the test of living. Life is an adventure of faith, if we are to be victors over it, not victims of it. Faith in the God above us, faith in the little infinite soul within us, faith in life and in our fellow souls — without faith, the plus quality, we cannot really live.

— JOSEPH FORT NEWTON

•

We must learn to be still in the midst of activity and to be vibrantly alive in repose.

— INDIRA GANDHI

The worst sin toward our fellow creatures is not to hate them, but to be indifferent to them: that's the essence of inhumanity.

— GEORGE BERNARD SHAW

♦

Points of View
We men are from one point of view mere trivial microbes, but from another the crown of creation: both views are true, and we must hold them together, interpenetrating, in our thought. From the point of view of the stellar universe, whose size and meaningless spaces baffle comprehension and belief, man may appear a mere nothing, and all his efforts destined to disappear like the web of a spider brushed down from the corner of a little room in the basement of a palace; but meanwhile he is engaged upon a task which by him can be imagined, the task of imposing mind and spirit upon matter and outer force. This he does by confronting the chaos of outer happenings with his intellect, and generating ordered knowledge; with his aesthetic sense, and generating beauty; with his purpose, and generating control of nature; with his ethical sense and his sense of humor, and generating character; with his reverence, and generating religion.

— JULIAN HUXLEY

Worry never robs tomorrow of its sorrow; it only saps today of its strength.

— A. J. CRONIN

♦

I deem nothing alien to my feelings that concerns a human being.

— TERENCE

♦

The Free Mind
I call that mind free which is not passively framed by outward circumstances, which is not swept away by the torrent of events, which is not the creature of accidental impulse, but which bends events to its own improvement, and acts from an inward spring, from immutable principles which it has deliberately espoused.

— WILLIAM ELLERY CHANNING

♦

Storms make oaks take deeper root.

— GEORGE HERBERT

♦

I find the great thing in this world is not so much where we stand as in what direction we are moving.

— OLIVER WENDELL HOLMES

The first key to wisdom is this—
constant and frequent questioning . . .
for by doubting we are led to question
and by questioning we arrive at the
truth.

— PETER ABELARD

Desert Places

Snow falling and night falling fast,
    oh, fast
In a field I looked into going past,
And the ground almost covered smooth
    in snow,
But a few weeds and stubble showing
    last.

The woods around it have it—it is
    theirs.
All animals are smothered in their lairs.
I am too absent-spirited to count;
The loneliness includes me unawares.

And lonely as it is that loneliness
Will be more lonely ere it will be less—
A blanker whiteness of benighted snow
With no expression, nothing to express.

They cannot scare me with their empty
    spaces
Between stars—on stars where no
    human race is.
I have it in me so much nearer home
To scare myself with my own desert
    places.

— ROBERT FROST

Heart-Throbs

Knowledge is happiness, because to have
knowledge—broad deep knowledge—is
to know true ends from false, and lofty
things from low. To know the thoughts
and deeds that have marked man's
progress is to feel the great heart-throbs
of humanity through the centuries; and
if one does not feel in these pulsations
a heavenward striving, one must indeed
be deaf to the harmonies of life.

— HELEN KELLER

Men are wise in proportion not to
their experience but to their capacity
for experience.

— GEORGE BERNARD SHAW

Integrity without knowledge is weak
and useless, and knowledge without
integrity is dangerous and dreadful.

— SAMUEL JOHNSON

Real charity and a real ability never to
condemn—the one real virtue—is so
often the result of a waking experience
that gives a glimpse of what lies beneath
things.

— IVY COMPTON-BURNETT

The farther backward you can look, the farther forward you are likely to see.

— WINSTON CHURCHILL

◆

No man is equipped for modern thinking until he has understood the anecdote of Agassiz and the fish.

A post-graduate student equipped with honours and diplomas went to [the naturalist] Agassiz to receive the final and finishing touches. The great man offered him a small fish and told him to describe it.

Post-Graduate Student: "That's only a sunfish."

Agassiz: "I know that. Write a description of it."

After a few minutes the student returned with the description of the Ichthus Heliodiplodkus, or whatever term is used to conceal the common sunfish from vulgar knowledge, the family of Heliichtherinkus, etc., as found in textbooks of the subject.

Agassiz again told the student to describe the fish.

The student produced a four-page essay. Agassiz again told him to look at the fish. At the end of three weeks the fish was in an advanced state of decomposition, but the student knew something about it.

— EZRA POUND

I think knowing what you can *not* do is more important than knowing what you can do. In fact, that's good taste.

— LUCILLE BALL

◆

The lowest ebb is the turn of the tide.

— HENRY WADSWORTH LONGFELLOW

◆

How [is one] to live a moral and compassionate existence when one is fully aware of the blood, darkness, the horror inherent in all life, when one finds darkness not only in one's culture but within oneself? If there is a stage at which an individual life becomes truly adult, it must be when one grasps the irony in its unfolding and accepts responsibility for a life lived in the midst of such paradox. One must live in the middle of contradiction because if all contradiction were eliminated at once life would collapse. There are simply no answers to come of the great pressing questions. You continue to live them out, making your life a worthy expression of leaning into the light.

— BARRY LOPEZ

◆

Most of the shadows of this life are caused by standing in one's own sunshine.

— RALPH WALDO EMERSON

Work

I never did anything worth doing by accident,
nor did any of my inventions come by accident;
they came by work.

Thomas A. Edison

The highest reward for man's toil is not what he gets for it but what he becomes by it.

—JOHN RUSKIN

•

Source of Happiness

So much unhappiness, it seems to me, is due to nerves; and bad nerves are the result of having nothing to do, or doing a thing badly, unsuccessfully or incompetently. Of all the unhappy people in the world, the unhappiest are those who have not found something they want to do. True happiness comes to him who does his work well, followed by a relaxing and refreshing period of rest. True happiness comes from the right amount of work for the day.

—LIN YUTANG

•

The things, good Lord, that we pray for, give us the grace to labour for.

—ST. THOMAS MORE

•

from L'Envoi

When Earth's last picture is painted,
    and the tubes are twisted and dried,
When the oldest colors have faded,
    and the youngest critic has died,
We shall rest, and, faith, we shall need
    it—lie down for an aeon or two,
Till the Master of All Good Workmen
    shall put us to work anew.

—RUDYARD KIPLING

Your Best Foot Forward

Which sounds longer to you, 569,400 hours or 65 years? They are exactly the same in length of time. The average man spends his first eighteen years— 157,000 hours—getting an education. That leaves him 412,000 hours from age 18 to 65. Eight hours of every day are spent in sleeping; eight hours in eating and recreation. So there is left eight hours to work in each day. One third of 412,000 hours is 134,000 hours—the number of hours a man has in which to work between the age of 18 and 65. Expressed in hours it doesn't seem a very long time, does it? Now I am not recommending that you tick off the hours that you worked, 134,000, 133,999, 133,998, etc., but I do suggest that whatever you do, you do it with all that you have in you. If you are sleeping, sleep well. If you are playing, play well. If you are working, give the best that is in you, remembering that in the last analysis the real satisfactions in life come not from money and things, but from the realization of a job well done. Therein lies the difference between the journeyman worker and a real craftsman.

—H. W. PRENTIS, JR.

•

Anyone can carry his burden, however hard, until nightfall. Anyone can do his work, however hard, for one day.

—ROBERT LOUIS STEVENSON

No man is born into the world
  whose work
Is not born with him; there is
  always work,
And tools to work withal, for
  those who will;
And blessed are the horny hands
  of toil!

    —JAMES RUSSELL LOWELL

♦

You cannot hope to build a better world without improving the individuals. To that end each of us must work for his own improvement, and at the same time show a general responsibility for all humanity, our particular duty being to aid those to whom we think we can be most useful.

    —MARIE CURIE

♦

Three Things are Needed

In order that people may be happy in their work, these three things are needed: they must be fit for it; they must not do too much of it; and they must have a sense of success in it—not a doubtful sense, such as needs some testimony of other people for its confirmation, but a sure sense, or rather knowledge, that so much work has been done well, and fruitfully done, whatever the world may say or think about it.

    —JOHN RUSKIN

Prayer and Work

Prayer is not a substitute for work; it is a desperate effort to work further and to be efficient beyond the range of one's powers. It is not the lazy who are most inclined to prayer; those pray most who care most, and who, having worked hard, find it intolerable to be defeated.

    —GEORGE SANTAYANA

♦

Work is doing what you now enjoy for the sake of a future which you clearly see and desire. Drudgery is doing under strain what you don't now enjoy and for no end that you can now appreciate.

    —RICHARD C. CABOT

♦

Nothing is really work unless you would rather be doing something else.

    —JAMES M. BARRIE

♦

Work is love made visible. And if you cannot work with love but only with distaste, it is better that you should leave your work and sit at the gate of the temple and take alms of those who work with joy. For if you bake bread with indifference, you bake a bitter bread that feeds but half man's hunger.

    —KAHLIL GIBRAN

The beauty of work depends upon the way we meet it, whether we arm ourselves each morning to attack it as an enemy that must be vanquished before night comes — or whether we open our eyes with the sunrise to welcome it as an approaching friend who will keep us delightful company and who will make us feel at evening that the day was well worth its fatigue.

— LUCY LARCOM

Good for the body is the work of the body, good for the soul is the work of the soul, and good for either is the work of the other.

— HENRY DAVID THOREAU

Don't worry and fret, faint-hearted,
    The chances have just begun,
For the best jobs haven't been started,
    The best work hasn't been done.

— BERTON BRALEY

St. Francis of Assisi was hoeing his garden when someone asked what he would do if he were suddenly to learn that he would die before sunset that very day. "I would finish hoeing my garden," he replied.

— LOUIS FISCHER

I long to accomplish a great and noble task, but it is my chief duty to accomplish humble tasks as though they were great and noble. The world is moved along, not only by the mighty shoves of its heroes, but also by the aggregate of the tiny pushes of each honest worker.

— HELEN KELLER

I can more easily see our Lord sweeping the streets of London than issuing edicts from its cathedral.

— DICK SHEPPARD

Be a gardener.
Dig a ditch,
toil and sweat,
and turn the earth upside down
and seek the deepness
and water the plants in time.
Continue this labor
and make sweet floods to run
and noble and abundant fruits
to spring.
Take this food and drink
and carry it to God
as your true worship.

— JULIAN OF NORWICH

Know that it is good to work. Work with love and think of liking it when you do it.

— BRENDA UELAND

Worship

The worship of God is not a rule of safety—
it is an adventure of the spirit,
a flight after the unattainable.

Alfred North Whitehead

If you want to know the closest place to
look for grace, it is within yourself.

— M. SCOTT PECK

◆

The Church of My Dreams

This is the church of my dreams:
The church of the warm heart,
Of the open mind,
Of the adventurous spirit;
The church that cares,
That heals hurt lives,
That comforts old people,
That challenges youth;
That knows no divisions of culture
    or class,
No frontiers, geographical or social;
The church that inquires as well
    as avers,
That looks forward as well as backward;
The church of the Master,
The church of the people,
High as the ideals of Jesus,
Low as the humblest human;
A working church,
A worshipping church,
A winsome church,
A church that interprets the truth in
    terms of truth,
That inspires courage for this life and
    hope for the life to come;
A church of courage
A church of all good men,
A church of the living God.

— JOHN MILTON MOORE

Benediction

Go on your way in peace.
Be of good courage.
Hold fast that which is good.
Render to no man evil for evil.
Strengthen the fainthearted.
Support the weak.
Help and cheer the sick.
Honor all men.
Love and serve the Lord.
May the blessing of God be upon you
    and remain with you forever.

— GLOUCESTER CATHEDRAL

◆

There is a little plant called reverence
in the corner of my soul's garden, which
I love to have watered once a week.

— OLIVER WENDELL HOLMES

◆

To be unknown of God is altogether too
much privacy.

— THOMAS MERTON

◆

On Entering Church

Pause ere thou enter, traveler, and
    bethink thee
How holy, yet how homelike, is this
    place;
Time that thou spendest humbly here
    shall link thee
With men unknown who once were
    of thy race.

— PLAQUE IN AN ENGLISH CHURCH

Every praying Christian, every person who has an encounter with God, must have a passionate concern for his or her brother and sister, his or her neighbor. To treat any one of these as if he were less than the child of God is to deny the validity of one's spiritual existence.

— DESMOND TUTU

♦

Greeting

Friend, you have come to this Church; leave it not without a prayer. No man entering a house ignores him who dwells in it. This is the House of God and He is here.

Pray then to Him who loves you and bids you welcome and awaits your greeting.

Give thanks for those who in past ages built this place to His glory and for those who, dying that we might live, have preserved for us our heritage.

Praise God for His gifts of beauty in painting and architecture, handicraft and music.

Ask that we who now live may build the spiritual fabric of the nation in truth, beauty, and goodness, and that as we draw near to the one Father through our Lord and Savior Jesus Christ we may draw nearer to one another in perfect brotherhood.

The Lord preserve thy going out and thy coming in.

— CANTERBURY CATHEDRAL

We should think of the church as an orchestra in which the different churches play on different instruments while a Divine Conductor calls the tune.

— WILLIAM R. INGE

♦

Sonnet

Oft have I seen at some cathedral door
   A laborer, pausing in the dust and
      heat,
   Lay down his burden, and with
      reverent feet
   Enter, and cross himself, and on
      the floor
Kneel to repeat his paternoster o'er;
   Far off the noises of the world retreat;
   The loud vociferations of the street
   Become an undistinguishable roar.
So, as I enter here from day to day,
   And leave my burden at this minster
      gate,
   Kneeling in prayer, and not ashamed
      to pray,
The tumult of the time disconsolate
   To inarticulate murmurs dies away,
   While the eternal ages watch and wait.

— HENRY WADSWORTH
                LONGFELLOW

♦

A man can no more diminish God's glory by refusing to worship him than a lunatic can put out the sun by scribbling "darkness" on the walls of his cell.

— C. S. LEWIS

My church helps me
  to keep a sky in my life and to look
    up,
  to keep my hand in God's and hold
    on to him,
  to see the eternal values above the
    material,
  to lift life above self to service for
    Christ,
  to see the good in others and praise it,
  to keep sweet and to keep busy for
    him,
  to have a seeing eye, a feeling heart,
    a helping hand,
  to test the motive of life and choose
    the best,
  to do justly, love mercy, and walk
    humbly.

— THE WATCHMAN-EXAMINER

♦

Ritual is the way we carry the presence
of the sacred. Ritual is the spark that
must not go out.

— CHRISTINA BALDWIN

♦

The Church in the Heart
Who builds a church within his heart
And takes it with him everywhere
Is holier far than he whose church
Is but a one-day house of prayer.

— MORRIS ABEL BEER

Worship
It is the soul searching for its counter-
    part.
It is a thirsty land crying out for rain.
It is a candle in the act of being kindled.
It is a drop in quest of the ocean.
It is a man listening through a tornado
    for the Still Small Voice.
It is a voice in the night calling for help.
It is a sheep lost in the wilderness
    pleading for rescue by the Good
    Shepherd.
It is the same sheep nestling in the arms
    of the rescuer.
It is the Prodigal Son running to his
    Father.
It is a soul standing in awe before the
    mystery of the Universe.
It is a poet enthralled by the beauty
    of a sunrise.
It is a workman pausing a moment to
    listen to a strain of music.
It is a hungry heart seeking for love.
It is a heart of love consecrating herself
    to her lover.
It is Time flowing into Eternity.
It is my little self engulfed in the
    Universal Self.
It is a man climbing the altar stairs
    to God.

— DWIGHT BRADLEY

♦

And what greater calamity can fall upon
a nation than the loss of worship.

— RALPH WALDO EMERSON

This Is My Church

A door
  into an opportunity for service,
  into the most useful life,
  into the best experience,
  into the most hopeful future—
  my church gives me a start.
An armory
  to get power to fight evil,
  to get inspiration to keep going right,
  to get an uplifting influence,
  to learn how to use spiritual weapons,
  to get a vision of Christ—
  my church keeps me moving.
An anchor
  to steady me in the storm,
  to keep me from the breakers,
  to guide me in the strenuous life,
  to hold me lest I drift away from God,
  to save me in the hour of temptation—
  and lead me into the harbor.

◆

Holiness

One should hallow all that one does in one's natural life. One eats in holiness, tastes the taste of food in holiness, and the table becomes an altar. One works in holiness, and he raises up the sparks which hide themselves in all tools. One walks in holiness across the fields, and the soft songs of all herbs, which they voice to God, enter into the song of our soul.

—MARTIN BUBER

Oh, to lie upon the rugs of some silent mosque, far from the noise of wanton city life, and, eyes closed, gaze turned heavenwards, listen to Islam's song forever!

—ISABELLE EBERHARDT

◆

When you walk across the fields with your mind pure and holy, then from all the stones, and all growing things, and all animals, the sparks of their soul come out and cling to you, and then they are purified and become a holy fire in you.

—HASIDIC SAYING

◆

Being a Christian is more than just an instantaneous conversion—it is a daily process whereby you grow to be more and more like Christ.

—BILLY GRAHAM

◆

Worship is the highest act of which man is capable. It not only stretches him beyond all the limits of his finite self to affirm the divine depth of mystery and holiness in the living and eternal God, but it opens him at the deepest level of his being to an act which unites him most realistically with his fellow man.

—SAMUEL H. MILLER

The Canticle of the Sun

O most high, almighty, good Lord God, to thee belong praise, glory,
honor, and all blessing!

Praised by my Lord God with all his creatures; and specially our
brother the sun, who brings us the day, and who brings us the
light; fair is he, and shining with a very great splendor: O Lord,
to us he signifies thee!

Praised be my Lord for our sister the moon, and for the stars, the
which he has set clear and lovely in heaven.

Praised be my Lord for our brother the wind, and for air and cloud,
calms and all weather, by the which thou upholdest in life all
creatures.

Praised be my Lord for our sister water, who is very serviceable unto
us, and humble, and precious, and clean.

Praised by my Lord for our brother fire, through whom thou givest
us light in the darkness; and he is bright, and pleasant, and very
mighty, and strong.

Praised be my Lord for our mother the earth, the which doth sustain
us and keep us, and bringeth forth divers fruits, and flowers of
many colors, and grass.

Praised be my Lord for all those who pardon one another for his
love's sake and who endure weakness and tribulation; blessed
are they who peaceably shall endure, for thou, O most Highest,
shalt give them a crown!

Praised be my Lord for our sister, the death of the body, from whom
no man escapeth. Woe to him who dieth in mortal sin! Blessed
are they who are found walking by thy most holy will, for the
second death shall have no power to do them harm.

Praise ye, and bless ye the Lord, and give thanks unto him, and serve
him with great humility.

—ST. FRANCIS OF ASSISI

Index of Authors

Index of First Lines of Poetry

Index of Topics

Acknowledgments

"A Song of Service," by Marguerite Few, from POEMS FOR DAILY NEEDS, edited by Thomas Curtis Clark (Harper & Row, Publishers).

"Desert Places" and "The Gift Outright," by Robert Frost, from THE POETRY OF ROBERT FROST, edited by Edward Connery Lathem. Copyright © 1936, 1942 by Robert Frost. Copyright © 1964, 1970 by Lesley Frost Ballantine. Copyright © 1969 by Henry Holt and Co., Inc. Reprinted by permission of Henry Holt and Co., Inc.

Extracts from THE PROPHET, by Kahlil Gibran. Copyright © 1923 by Kahlil Gibran and renewed 1951 by Administrators C.T.A. of Kahlil Gibran Estate and Mary G. Gibran. Reprinted by permission of Alfred A. Knopf, Inc.

"Two Prayers," by Andrew Gillies, from MASTER-PIECES OF RELIGIOUS VERSE, edited by James Dalton Morrison (Harper & Row, Publishers).

"Loveliest of Trees," from THE COLLECTED POEMS OF A. E. HOUSMAN. Used by permission of The Society of Authors as the literary representative of A. E. Housman.

"Outwitted," by Edwin Markham, from POEMS OF EDWIN MARKHAM, edited by Charles L. Wallis (Harper & Row, Publishers).

"The Ways," by John Oxenham, from SELECTED POEMS OF JOHN OXENHAM, edited by Charles L. Wallis (Harper & Row, Publishers).

"Night Journey," © 1940 by Theodore Roethke, from THE COLLECTED POEMS OF THEODORE ROETHKE. Used by permission of Doubleday, a division of Bantam Doubleday Dell Publishing Group, Inc.

"Prayer for Strength," from GITANJALI, by Rabindranath Tagore (New York: Collier Books, 1971). Reprinted with permission of Collier Books, an imprint of Simon & Schuster Inc.

"Barter," by Sara Teasdale, from COLLECTED POEMS OF SARA TEASDALE (New York: Macmillan, 1937). Reprinted with permission of Scribner, a Division of Simon & Schuster Inc.

"A Blessing," from COLLECTED POEMS, by James Wright. Copyright © 1971 by James Wright, Wesleyan University Press by permission of University Press of New England.

"When You Are Old," by William Butler Yeats, from THE POEMS OF W. B. YEATS: A NEW EDITION, edited by Richard J. Finneran (New York: Macmillan, 1983). Reprinted with permission of Scribner, a Division of Simon & Schuster Inc.